T0305662

Culture Matters

Decision-Making in Global Virtual Teams

Culture Matters

Decision-Making in Global Virtual Teams

Norhayati Zakaria

CRC Press
Taylor & Francis Group
Boca Raton London New York

CRC Press is an imprint of the
Taylor & Francis Group, an **informa** business

CRC Press
Taylor & Francis Group
6000 Broken Sound Parkway NW, Suite 300
Boca Raton, FL 33487-2742

First issued in paperback 2021

ISBN-13: 978-1-4822-4016-0 (hbk)
ISBN-13: 978-1-03-217935-3 (pbk)
DOI: 10.1201/9781315372976

Library of Congress Cataloging-in-Publication Data

Names: Norhayati Zakaria, 1969- author.
Title: Culture matters : decision-making in global virtual teams / Norhayati Zakaria.
Description: Boca Raton, FL : CRC Press, 2017.
Identifiers: LCCN 2016025946 | ISBN 9781482240160 (hardback : alk. paper)
Subjects: LCSH: Virtual work teams. | Decision making--Cross-cultural studies. | Intercultural communication. | Management--Cross-cultural studies.
Classification: LCC HD66 .N665 2017 | DDC 658.4/022--dc23
LC record available at https://lccn.loc.gov/2016025946

Visit the Taylor & Francis Web site at
http://www.taylorandfrancis.com

and the CRC Press Web site at
http://www.crcpress.com

Contents

Foreword

Virtual Harmony amid Cultural Dissonance

The meaning and means to work together have forever changed with the advent of the Internet. Teamwork and collaboration no longer require geographic proximity or even the same time zone. New technologies enable us to reach across the global divide and work together virtually without being hampered by distance or space—it is a great new world of work—or is it?

Are *global virtual teams* (GVTs, in short) the perfect tool for this perfect new technologically enhanced global workplace, or are there still challenges that teams must face even when the global divide is broached?

What hampers, hinders, or facilitates GVT success are the key questions that Dr. Norhayati Zakaria, an expert in the study of GVTs, continues to address in her writings and research since she first delved into this new world of inquiry nearly 20 years ago. A keen observer of the advantages and challenges this new connectivity brings to the global workplace, Dr. Zakaria brings to the fore the importance of culture and cultural influences on all aspects of GVT interactions.

In *Culture Matters: Decision-Making in Global Virtual Teams*, Dr. Zakaria provides a clear, articulate examination of the significance of cultural influences on team decision-making processes and team determination outcomes.

By addressing how the distinct cultural norms held by individual team members influence communication protocols, the perceptions of task and relationship importance, and the concepts of time, which, in turn, impact team relations, cohesion, and efficacy, Dr. Zakaria amply demonstrates the need for managers to gain cross-cultural competencies and effective strategies in order to manage productive GVTs.

Culture Matters offers managers, students, and scholars alike a highly readable and accessible narrative that effectually explains why GVTs pose a variety of new managerial and organizational challenges while likewise providing organizations with a tremendous new and potentially rewarding team structure *when managed well*, as Dr. Zakaria so clearly states.

Dr. Zakaria's book is exceptional in that it bridges the gap between scholars and practitioners by providing a thorough comprehensive analysis of why culture matters for GVTs and synthesizing the challenges of managing effective GVTs, as well as providing practical strategies (*dos and don'ts*) on how to manage GVTs. In this context, Dr. Zakaria points out that technological tools alone are insufficient, and it is imperative to better understand how technology and cultural influences interact and shape globally distributed collaboration in order to lead successful GVTs.

Culture Matters is a book that addresses what culture is and why it matters in a world of globally distributed entities endeavoring to be productive and responsive to internal and external exigencies. Dr. Zakaria has succeeded admirably in presenting a framework for understanding why cross-cultural differences within a team impact the GVT performance and

providing worthwhile recommendations for GVT management
and performance enhancement.

Andrea Amelinckx, J.D.
Director, International Management Program
Faculty of Management
University of Lethbridge
Lethbridge, Alberta, Canada

Preface

Culture is communication and communication is culture.

Edward T. Hall
1976, p. 191

Culture? Yes...Culture!

I am and have always been passionate about culture. At the same time, my mind is stimulated and provoked with endless curiosity about the meaning of *culture* and its impact on human behavior in life, as well as in the workplace. I believe that one's behavior at work is rooted in one's cultural values. On the other hand, workplace practices, rituals, and routines can further shape one's own cultural values. More than a decade ago, I began to craft my research on culturally oriented organizational behaviors, also known as cross-cultural management. Unsurprisingly, then, when I embarked on my PhD journey in 2001 in the School of Information Studies at Syracuse University, I chose to study culture. That was all I wanted to do, and that was exactly what I ended up doing. From day one, I told my peers and my professors that I would study culture. Some gave me a strange look; some gave me an approving look. Some said, "It's too early to think of a topic," while some said, "That's good, you're already clear about what you want to do." Despite such conflicting remarks, I continued to craft my research topic, finding ways to verify that such study is needed and worth it, adamant to stamp my PhD topic with the word culture.

It is challenging to study culture, since the concept itself has been defined by scholars in more than 160 ways. The key question often pointed out to me during intellectual discourse was "How do you measure culture, or how do you explain and describe such an intricate concept?"

Certainly, culture oftentimes carries intangible meanings that are abstract and difficult to comprehend or analyze. Culture is an abstract concept with many varied definitions (Ferraro 2003; Schneider & Barsoux 1997; Kroeber & Kluckhohn 1952). In this book, I define culture as a pattern of behaviors that are shared by a group of people (i.e., from a shared national identity, ethnicity, or race) that rests on basic assumptions. The basic assumption used in this study is drawn from Hall's (1976) cultural dimension called *context*. In terms of cultural communication, context has two poles, high context (HC) and low context (LC), to distinguish between context-oriented and content-oriented communication. HC people emphasize the nonverbal aspects of communication (body language, tone of voice, situation, etc.), whereas LC people emphasize the verbal aspects of communication (words alone, written, or spoken).

Examining the impact of culture on behavior has provoked me to consider many questions, such as what, why, who, when, and how a person thinks, feels, and behaves due to the effects of culture. It has inspired me to discover the cognitive elements of a human brain and then explore the emotional state of a person's feelings in order to justify why a certain action or behavior is fully demonstrated or implied. Thus, the challenge is how to capture all these questions and how to explore them on such a variable dimension. My curious mind then went further: why does culture influence our behavior in the workplace? Does culture matter differently in different management roles, in particular, for processes such as decision making? In what ways does culture influence the decision-making process when it takes place in a distributed form, such as GVTs?

I began my research journey by exploring culture using a unique research context: the virtual workspace. I had three reasons for doing so. First, one consequence of globalization has been a high mobility of employees, which has changed the landscape and structure of the workplace. Globalization liberates people to move across borders wherever and whenever they desire in order to be employed. Similar patterns can be observed in the movement of goods and services that are free to be transported, exported, and imported worldwide. Second, with the widespread availability of new and more advanced technological and social media tools, the work setting has been transformed into a different structure and has taken different forms for both work and play. Third, the distributed work setting resulting from this, also known as the virtual workspace, allows people to be *collocated* with other team members without the need to travel and to work together despite barriers of geographical space, different time zones, and diverse cultural values. The common mantra of GVTs is *anywhere, anytime, and with anyone.*

However, as might be expected with such an innovative work structure, many challenges arise, and many questions are left unanswered. One of these questions is "How do you manage far-flung human resources when they are collaborating and working at a distance?"

The structure of this book is divided into five sections, comprising 17 chapters. The introduction explains the motivation for writing the book and outlines its structure. In Section I, I present the phenomenon of anywhere, anytime, and with anyone to highlight the prevalence of the virtual workplace in contemporary multinational or international organizations and discuss the research background, which has its roots in one subgroup as the GVTs of Civil Society during the World Summit on the Information Society.

In Section II, I define the concept of culture by providing an overview in understanding between three different levels of human mental programming that clearly denote culture as a group phenomenon, not specific to an individual or encompassing the universal human needs. I further explain the distinctive characteristics of culture through an *onion model*, which has three different layers—(1) artifacts and symbols, (2) norms and values, and (3) basic assumptions and behaviors. It is important to clearly understand the concept with its many layers as it helps us to understand the multifaceted behaviors of people at the workplace, particularly during the decision-making process. Under this section, the book also provides two distinctive theoretical lenses to ground the understanding of cultural impacts on the distributed decision-making process— Edward Hall's (1976) high context versus low context and Fons Trompenaars's (1993) seven dimensions.

Section III discusses the decision-making process by integrating two perspectives. First, I looked at Kingdon's decision-making model, which highlights the political decision process. Second, I applied Adler's (1997) decision-making model to further explain the cultural influence on such process. As a result, I presented an empirical model of a distributed decision-making process that integrates both Kingdon's and Adler's model, which is unique to the environment of GVTs. Based on the findings, the study concludes that the distributed decisions made by the team members are based on a cyclical model that is more iterative and dynamic as compared to a sequential process that is suggested by Kingdon.

Section IV further refines the understanding on the distributed decision-making process by considering specific cultural elements. Adler's model suggests that every aspect of the decision-making process is much attuned to the cultural values that belong either in a society or in a group. Therefore, under this section, I present several chapters that illustrate the impacts of cultural values on decision making such as individualism versus communitarianism and task oriented versus relationship oriented. Another aspect would be focused on the intercultural communication styles that examine the impact of directness versus indirectness and detailed versus ambiguous on the way that people communicate in the email discussions for proposing ideas; highlighting problems; deliberating the ideas, problems, and issues; and then arriving at a decision.

Finally, in Section V, I provide several implications that are critical for multinational organizations in order to achieve, as well as sustain, high-performing GVTs. Undeniably, in the current global work environment, many multinational corporations or international-based organizations thrive on virtual workspace and virtual structure to capitalize their global human resources. As the prevailing strategic plans, GVTs assemble synergistic members across the world to collaborate hand in hand to meet organizational goals. At the same time, by utilizing GVTs, companies can reap profits from their much-reduced costs because of the elimination of travelling expenses and the cost of failure in expatriation. Thus, I will include three chapters on the *know-how* or the dos and don'ts in working in a virtual workspace, the reasons and motivation to develop cross-cultural competencies, and ways to strategically manage the impacts of the cultural values' differences on the distributed decision-making process. As a conclusion, the book offers an affirmation that *culture counts* even at a distance in the globally distributed collaboration phenomenon.

References

Adler, N.J. 1997. *International Dimensions of Organizational Behavior*, 3rd ed. Cincinnati, OH: South-Western.

Ferraro, G.P. 2003. *The Cultural Dimension of International Business*. Upper Saddle River, NJ: Prentice Hall.

Hall, E.T. 1976. *Beyond Culture*. Garden City, NJ: Anchor Books/ Doubleday.

Kroeber, A.L. & Kluckhohn, C. 1952. Culture: A critical review of concepts and definitions. Retrieved October 13, 2015, available at http://www.scribd.com/doc/230913406/Kroeber-y-Kluckhohn-1952-Culture-a-critical-review-of-concepts-and-definitions#scribd.

Schneider, S.C. & Barsoux, J. 1997. *Managing Across Cultures*. London: Prentice Hall.

Trompenaars, F. 1993. *Riding the Waves of Culture: Understanding Cultural Diversity in Business*. London: Economist Books.

Acknowledgments

Bismi-Allahi Ar-Rahmani, Ar-Raheem

With Allah's willing, after many years, I have finally managed to turn my dissertation into a book. It took me two years to finish this challenging journey of turning my research findings on global virtual teams and culture into practical implications that, I hope, will be useful to scholars and practitioners. Neither the research nor the book-writing journey would have been possible without the countless help, guidance, and support of my beloved people around me: my beloved spouse—Associate Professor Dr. Shafiz Affendi Mohd Yusof, my parents and in-laws, family members, and colleagues. Let me also extend my deepest appreciation to my former advisor, Dr. Derrick L. Cogburn, who has been instrumental in making the PhD journey less painful and more successful. He has been extremely supportive both as a friend and as a mentor. My deepest appreciation also goes to my committee members: Dr. Ruth Small, who has been a source of motivation to me and has often said, "You can do it!" with a reassuring look, Dr. Michelle Kaarst-Brown, who has been a friend and has offered a helping hand over many wonderful lunches, and Dr. Carsten Osterlund, who offered a listening ear and said, "You just have to do it." Additionally, I owe a debt to my readers, Dr. Milton Mueller and Dr. David Wilemon, who have diligently read my drafts and dissertation and provided constructive comments. Not forgetting, a dear friend, Dr. Emilie Gould, who has been my teacher and a good friend over the years, thank you for believing in me; my editor—Michele Rothen—who has helped me clarify what I wanted to say in a more concise manner; my IST-Syracuse University friends, especially the *Golden Girls—our reading club,* which tremendously supported me; my research assistant—Nursakirah Ab Rahman Muton—who turned the drafts into the right format, and my long-term virtual international research partner, Andrea Amelinckx, at the University of Lethbridge, Canada for working *in sync* with me despite being thousands of miles apart.

About the Author

Dr. Norhayati Zakaria is an associate professor at the Faculty of Business and Management at the University of Wollongong in Dubai. Dr. Zakaria earned both her PhD degree in information science and technology and MPhil degree in information transfer at Syracuse University, and her MSc degree in management at Rensselaer Polytechnic Institute, Troy. Her research expertise combines several interdisciplinary fields, including cross-cultural management, international business, and computer-mediated communication technology. For more than a decade, Dr. Zakaria has established international research collaborations with global scholars from the United States, Japan, and Canada. As a principal investigator, she has obtained international research grants from the Asian Office of Aerospace Research & Development (AOARD). Since 2006, she has been serving as a senior research faculty associate at the Center for Research on Collaboratories and Technology Enhanced Learning Communities (COTELCO) under American University, where she led projects using global virtual teams. All her research works are built on a qualitative research method in which she believes provides illuminating results with deep insights and rich descriptions of culturally attuned phenomenon at workplace face-to-face or virtually. Since she has been trained in the Western educational system, actively engaged in international research collaborations, and has experiences in teaching at the Middle Eastern region, she has developed eminent cross-cultural competencies with vast global experiences.

GLOBAL VIRTUAL TEAM

Indeed, we are on a different time zone!

Goodness, what time is it? As Mr. Takamura Yama looked at the clock, he felt relieved that it is only 4 p.m. and that he can still send a document to his team member in Delhi—Mr. Pravant Prabu, a senior engineer in Panasonic. Yet, the documents will not be read by their team member in Chicago as he is fast asleep. Perhaps, Mr. David Samuel will reply tomorrow once he reads it. But, all the team members need to agree on the proposal and send confirmation by 10 a.m. the next day. Mr. Takamura feels so anxious that they might not make it to the 9 a.m. deadline since he needs to send it to his Tokyo headquarters. As he sighed, he thought, "How could this happen?" and instantly felt frustrated for not incorporating the difference in time zone when planning his work.

Chapter 1

Anywhere, Anytime, and with Anyone— Virtual Workplace

Introduction

In a virtual workspace, people still need to make decisions as efficiently as usual, despite the geographical distance. Most of the time, teams are challenged with a different working time zone. It can range from as minimal as an hour (Malaysia versus Japan) to an extreme of 12 hours apart (Malaysia versus United States). Communication is thus heavily reliant on technology to speed up decisions. Additionally, team members are culturally divergent in their working practices, values, and attitudes. Thus, the key question is, when working together, how can team members collaborate effectively when they are faced with different cultural values, time zones, and remote geographical locations? Rapid globalization and the advancement of information communication technology (ICT) have resulted in a new, effective, and efficient workplace phenomenon. With the proliferate use of ICT, the virtual workplace has totally changed the normal work orientation and space

3

in multinational corporations (Gibson et al. 2014; Gilson et al. 2014). As such, the mark of the 21st century has made it possible for people to fully seize the advantage of this new form of global collaboration as it provides opportunities for people to work with anyone, anywhere, and any time.

ICT entails greater efforts to manage globally distributed collaboration across the world. Globally distributed collaboration often takes place through computer-mediated communication (CMC) technologies, many of which rely heavily on the Internet and complex information systems. Globally distributed collaboration also demands managing intercultural communication, defined as interaction between people of diverse cultural backgrounds with distinct communication patterns, preferences, and styles. On the one hand, CMC allows people to communicate and collaborate unrestricted by barriers of time and space. On the other hand, cultural barriers stemming from different managerial aspects and communication styles may adversely affect various elements of collaboration such as negotiations, deliberation of ideas, self-disclosure, conflict resolution, coordination, and so on (Rusman et al. 2010; Paul et al. 2004). Potential culture-related management problem areas include overcoming high anxiety and the uncertainty of feelings (Germain & McGuire 2014; Hertel et al. 2005), managing conflicting and frustrating situations (Dickinson 2013; Holt & DeVore 2005), saving face in confrontational situations (Ting-Toomey 1997), making effective group decisions (Oetzel 2005), diverse leadership style (Hill et al. 2014; Huang et al. 2010), using language and nonverbal communication (Lockwood 2015; Lee 2009; Shachaf 2008), and adjusting to and acculturating in a new environment (Lu et al. 2011; Smith & Khawaja 2011; Haslberger 2010).

The use of CMC among people with different cultural values can either facilitate or impede collaboration and communication (Hill et al. 2014; Shen et al. 2014). Early scholars of CMC suggested that it is ineffective in several areas (e.g., establishing online relationships, producing effective communication, and expressing oneself or receiving feedback) due to the absence of contextual, visual, and aural cues (Magnusson et al. 2014; Gu et al. 2011; Ramirez, Jr. et al. 2002; Wachter 1999; Daft & Lengel 1984). For example, electronic mail (email) is referred to as a *lean media* because it relies purely on textual elements. For people whose intercultural communication styles rely heavily on nonverbal or paralinguistic cues (tone of voice, facial expressions, body movements, and gestures) to interpret the information they receive, lean media was believed to pose a significant barrier to effective communication. With the range of cultural values, managing this new form of collaboration and communication in a distributed environment using CMC becomes more challenging and intense. Essentially, the challenges arise because, as Hall (1976) asserted, high-context culture prefers nonverbal cues, whereas email lacks such key characteristic.

The unresolved question, therefore, is, how does culture impact participation in the distributed environment, particularly the decision-making process, when people use CMC technologies to participate and collaborate? The significance of this book lies in its exploration and description of the cultural factors that influenced the participation of global virtual teams collaborating via email, and in its investigation into whether different cultural orientations gave rise to different communicative behaviors, thus impacting the way or manner individuals contributed to the decision-making processes. In this regard, the book will describe cultural variations such as intercultural communication styles, individualism versus collectivism, and task versus relationship orientation during the decision-making process. From Hall's theoretical lens and literature support, people who employ high-context cultural communication styles have different ways of making proposals, deliberating on ideas, making choices, and coming up with solutions from people who employ low-context cultural communication styles.

Case 1: Cultural Vignette

Working at a Distance, Working with Culture

Adam Resnick, the regional manager at the headquarters of South Western Inc. in Utah, sat in his office contemplating one crucial question: how will he lead a negotiation and collaboration effort involving team members in three different parts of the world? Over the course of a ten-week project, a team of Indian engineers needs to collaborate with Swedish engineers to develop microcomputer products and then communicate with a Malaysian marketing manager on the exporting of the products to Southeast Asia. Adam is perplexed. "How is this possible when they will have no opportunities to meet and have no history of working together?," he wonders.

As an American, Adam's usual way of working is to develop plans, coordinate, and implement tasks based on structured milestones and datelines. The moment he learned he would need to complete the task within ten weeks, he was full of plans and ideas on how to coordinate the tasks according to weekly goals and develop a strategy to execute it. With all his planning documents ready, he is ready to make the team effort a success, so he sends out an introductory email to his colleagues in India, Sweden, and Malaysia. In the message, he introduces himself, informs them about the task at hand, and elaborates on his plans to carry out the project successfully. At the end of the email, he says, "I will oversee the project and ensure that all the tasks will be carried out efficiently and as planned."

Prakash and Ainuddin, the Indian engineers on the team, are taken by surprise when they receive the long email full of instructions and guidelines from their project manager. They had not expected to need to get to work immediately, considering that they still have two months to go in the project. Although both of them are well aware that they have a short time to complete the task, which is quite demanding, they were expecting Adam to call or send a short, friendly email to get the project rolling. They were hoping that the email would give them information about him, his position, and his role in the project. As Ainuddin comments to his colleague, "I got an email that tells me to stay focused—it is almost like the task is already being executed, and no joke!" On the other hand, Carlsten, the Swedish architect, is extremely happy to see such careful plans laid out. He is motivated to give his best efforts to get the project completed on time.

As the project moves into its third week, confusion arises, and there are many instances of miscommunication. Ainuddin is frustrated because he does not understand what is going on, but he is hesitant to ask questions because he does not want to expose his lack of knowledge. At the same time, Adam is annoyed that Prakash is relenting over the impressive developments, but he does not see any tasks being completed as expected. All the deadlines he has set have been missed. Although he sent out many reminders and was adamant about getting everyone on the same page, he received no replies. After a couple of days, Ainuddin might briefly mention his progress (and Prakash's responses were always positive), but nothing has been delivered. And yet Carlsten seems to have no trouble adhering to the deadlines. As the end of the project approaches, Adam starts to wonder, "Which is the real challenge in managing global virtual teams? Working at a distance? Or working with their cultural differences?"

References

Daft, R.L. & Lengel, R.H. 1984. Information richness: A new approach to managerial behavior and organizational design. In L.L. Cummings & B.M. Staw (Eds.), *Research in Organizational Behavior*, 6 (pp. 191–233). Homewood, IL: JAI Press.

Dickinson, J.B. 2013. An examination of multi-dimensional channel conflict: A proposed experimental approach. *Journal of Behavioral Studies in Business*. Retrieved January 27, 2016, available at http://www.aabri.com/manuscripts/121244.pdf.

Germain, M.I. & McGuire, D. 2014. The role of swift trust in virtual teams and implications for human resource development. *Advances in Developing Human Resources*, 16(3), 356–370.

Gibson, C.B., Huang, L., Kirkman, B.L. & Shapiro, D.L. 2014. Where global and virtual meet: The value of examining the intersection of these elements in twenty-first-century teams. *Annual Review of Organizational Psychology and Organizational Behavior*, 1(1), 217–244.

Gilson, L.L., Maynard, M.T., Young, N.C.J., Vartiainen, M. & Hakonen, M. 2014. Virtual teams research: 10 years, 10 themes, and 10 opportunities. *Journal of Management*, 41(5), 1313–1337.

Gu, R., Higa, K. & Moodie, D.R. 2011. A study on communication media selection: Comparing the effectiveness of the media richness, social influence, and media fitness. *Journal of Service Science Management*, 4(3), 291–299.

Hall, E.T. 1976. *Beyond Culture*. Garden City, NJ: Anchor Books/ Doubleday.

Haslberger, A. 2010. Gender differences and expatriate adjustment. *European Journal of International Management*, 4(10), 163–183.

Hertel, G., Geister, S. & Konradt, U. 2005. Managing virtual teams: A review of current empirical research. *Human Resource Management Review*, 15(1), 69–95.

Hill, N.S., Lorinkova, N. & Karaca, A. 2014. A critical review and meta-analysis of leadership behaviors and virtual teams performance. *Academy of Management Proceedings*, 1, 12990–12990.

Holt, J.L. & DeVore, C.J. 2005. Culture, gender, organizational role, and styles of conflict resolution: A meta-analysis. *International Journal of Intercultural Relations*, 29(1), 165–196.

Huang, R., Kahai, S. & Jestice, R. 2010. The contingent effects of leadership on team collaboration in virtual teams. *Computers in Human Behavior*, 26(5), 1098–1110.

Lee, M.R. 2009. E-ethical leadership for virtual project teams. *International Journal of Project Management*, 27(5), 456–463.

Lockwood, J. 2015. Virtual team management: What's causing communication breakdown? *Language & Intercultural Communication*, 15(1), 125–140.

Lu, Y., Samaratunge, R. & Hartel, C. 2011. Acculturation strategies among professional Chinese immigrants in the Australian workplace. *Asia Pacific Journal of Human Resources*, 49(1), 71–87.

Magnusson, P., Schuster, A. & Taras, V. 2014. A process-based explanation of the psychic distance paradox: Evidence from global virtual teams. *Management International Review*, 54(3), 283–306.

Oetzel, J.G. 2005. Effective intercultural workgroup communication theory. In W.B. Gudykunst (Ed.), *Theorizing About Intercultural Communication* (pp. 351–372). Thousand Oaks, CA: SAGE.

Paul, S., Seetharaman, P., Samarah, I. & Mykytyn, P.P. 2004. Impact of heterogeneity and collaborative conflict management style on the performance of synchronous global virtual teams. *Information & Management*, 41(3), 303–321.

Ramirez, Jr., A., Walther, J.B., Burgoon, J.K. & Sunnafrank, M. 2002. Information seeking strategies, uncertainty, and computer-mediated communication: Toward a conceptual model. *Human Communication Research*, 28, 213–228.

Rusman, E., van Bruggen, J. Sloep, P. & Koper, R. 2010. Fostering trust in virtual project teams: Towards a design framework grounded in a Trustworthiness Antecedents (TWAN) schema. *International Journal of Human-Computer Studies*, 68(11), 834–850.

Shachaf, P. 2008. Cultural diversity and information and communication technology impacts on global virtual teams: An exploratory study. *Information & Management*, 45(2), 131–142.

Shen, Z., Lyytinen, K. & Yoo, Y. 2014. Time and information technology in teams: A review of empirical research and future research directions. Forthcoming in *European Journal of Information Systems*, 24(5), 492–518.

Smith, R.A. & Khawaja, N.G. 2011. A review of the acculturation experiences of international students. *International Journal of Intercultural Relations*, 35, 699–713.

Ting-Toomey, S. 1997. Intercultural conflict competence. In W. Cupach & D. Canary (Eds.), *Competence in Interpersonal Conflict* (pp. 120–147). New York: McGraw-Hill.

Wachter, R.M. 1999. The effect of gender and communication mode on conflict resolution. *Computers in Human Behavior*, 15(1), 763–782.

Chapter 2

What Is a Global Virtual Team?

Introduction

In the management field, a team is defined as a small col-
lection of people at work who engage in interpersonal interactions to achieve established goals (Piccoli et al. 2004).
According to Johnson and Johnson (1997), they define a team
as two or more individuals with the following elements and
characteristics: (a) members are interdependent and strive to
achieve mutual goals; (b) they need to communicate in order
to achieve the stated and agreed goals; (c) members are cognizant of the members' contributions—who is contributing
and who is not; (d) members are assigned with specific tasks,
roles, and responsibilities; (e) and the life span of membership
is limited because members are usually assembled on an
ad-hoc basis.

Teams are an important means of engaging an organization's
creative and problem-solving capabilities. For an organization to
be competitive and resourceful, they need teams that can create
synergies among coworkers. Eliciting ideas from several minds
often leads to more creative solutions than one person working

on a task alone. As the saying goes, "Alone we can do so little, together we can do so much!" (Helen Keller, American political activist). Kenneth Blanchard supported this idea in his well-known book *The One Minute Manager* (1982), in which he says, "None of us is as smart as all of us."

The development of computer-mediated communication (CMC) technology and its introduction into multinational corporations (MNCs) have given rise to a different form of teamwork called global virtual teams (GVTs). To fully exploit this novel work structure, MNCs also need to develop new practices, procedures, standards, and tasks for teams that depend on CMC technologies for their daily work routines. This phenomenon is known as the *digital-wave workspace* and is becoming prevalent in MNCs.

According to Jarvenpaa and Leidner (1999), GVTs have three characteristics: (1) they are culturally diverse, (2) they are geographically dispersed, and (3) team members use electronic technology (e.g., email) to communicate. Jarvenpaa and Leidner (1999) define GVTs as an ad-hoc or temporary team in which team members do not have a shared history of working together as a group and are unlikely to do so again in the future. Yusof and Zakaria (2012) further suggest that GVTs can be defined as teams that (1) are noncollocated and thus can work across different organizational boundaries, functionalities, and/or geographical locations; (2) use information communication technology (asynchronous and/or synchronous) to collaborate and communicate for work purposes; (3) experience time zone differences; (4) work on tasks or projects that allow temporally flexible schedules; and (5) have team members from diverse cultural backgrounds.

For all of these reasons, GVTs can present complex and varied challenges. For example, imagine working with strangers, without any knowledge of their past performance by which to judge their reliability and trustworthiness. Imagine engaging with team members for extended work hours or even during normally off-work hours due to being in different time zones. Imagine dealing with diverse communication styles, decision-making patterns, negotiation approaches, and leadership traits because team members come from different cultural backgrounds. Imagine trying to defuse a conflict when collaboration and competition are interpreted differently because of culturally rooted values, attitudes, and perceptions.

In order for MNCs to have high-performing GVTs, they must rely heavily on CMC, since geographical distance is no longer a barrier to virtual cross-border collaboration. However, coping with cultural diversity in a work setting requires different skills—for example, building trust is an essential element in team effectiveness (Zakaria & Yusof 2015; Klitmoller & Lauring 2013), but cultural diversity can either promote or hinder the formation of swift trust in a virtual work environment (Branzei et al. 2007). In addition, it is important to note that the extent of virtualness varies (Solomon 2012; Kirkman et al. 2004; Zigurs 2003) and depends largely on the need and nature of the collaborative work being undertaken.

The degree of virtualness has two elements: (1) level of communication and (2) time spent working apart (Griffith & Neale 2001). As shown in Figure 2.1, pure virtual teams (upper right) never meet face to face regardless of the communication tools that are used. At the other extreme (lower left) are traditional or face-to-face teams that do not use any CMC tools at all. Given the current state of technology and globalization, both extremes are nearly nonexistent (Griffith et al. 2003). The hybrid environment or hybrid collaboration is most common, where communication takes place face to face, as well as virtually (Nunamaker et al. 1998; Warkentin et al. 1997).

These several definitions of GVTs suggest that team members differ not only in the degree of virtuality (as shown by their use of information and communication technologies as their primary means of communication) but also in terms of their national and cultural backgrounds. Consequently, I define GVTs as separated by time and space but, more

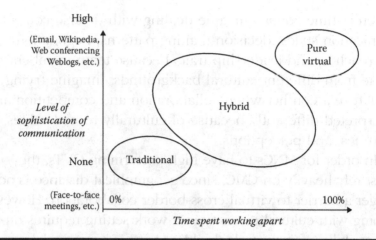

Figure 2.1 Dimensions of virtualness. (Adapted from Griffith, T.L. & Neale, M.A., Informational processing in traditional, hybrid, and virtual teams: From nascent knowledge to transactive memory, in B.M. Staw & R.I. Sutton (Eds.), *Research in Organizational Behavior: An Annual Series of Analytical Essays and Critical Reviews*, 23 (pp. 379–421), 2001.)

importantly, as differing in national, cultural, and linguistic attributes and work structure.

Case 2: Cultural Vignette

You Speak Differently! Diverse Communication Styles

After working with her virtual team for almost ten days, Ms. Kim Hue, a promising young architect from Vietnam, is feeling upset and stressed. This makes her contemplate whether or not her energy and effort have been a waste of time. When a colleague asks her, "What has happened to you? I no longer hear about your enthusiasm and optimism about the eight-week project, are you doing OK?" Kim starts to express her frustration. "It was fantastic in the beginning since all five of my team members from Sweden, the

U.S. and Germany was so cooperative. Moreover, considering I am only a junior executive among them, I can tell that they appreciate and respect my ideas as they often support and encourage me to share ideas. I was highly motivated to contribute—to the extent that I said 'Yes' whenever they wanted to have meetings late at night or even at two or three in the morning for me, due to the time difference. But yesterday my team leader, Mr. Grisham Anthony, the Swedish guy, sent me a long and harsh email about the problems we encountered. I was shocked and don't know what to do. He confronted me directly about the issues and he did it in a public space (using email). I am ashamed and embarrassed." Kim values her privacy and normally employs a subtle or indirect way of addressing a problem. She always tries to avoid confrontation out of a desire to save face by not embarrassing people publicly. What her leader did is unacceptable and upsetting to her, so much so that she says to her boss, Mr. Duong Hou, "If things don't seem to work out, I will quit this project." Duong listens carefully to her account of what has happened, then says to her, "Kim, the way Westerners speak is direct and straightforward. That is just the way they communicate. It isn't mean to be aggressive or rude. You and I, on the other hand, tend to keep to ourselves. My advice is to ignore it, and continue to work as diligently as you have. After all, I chose you since you are the best we have!" With that reassurance, Kim sighs to herself, "Well this is a real challenge for me since I cannot see their facial expressions or hear their tone of voice via email. But perhaps it is just part and parcel of teamwork!"

References

Branzei, O., Vertinsky, I. & Camp, I.I. 2007. Culture-contingent signs of trust in emergent relationships. *Organizational Behavior and Human Decision Processes*, 104, 61–82.

Griffith, T.L. & Neale, M.A. 2001. Informational processing in traditional, hybrid, and virtual teams: From nascent knowledge to transactive memory. In B.M. Staw & R.I. Sutton (Eds.), *Research in Organizational Behavior: An Annual Series of Analytical Essays and Critical Reviews*, 23 (pp. 379–421).

Griffith, T.L., Sawyer, J.E. & Neale, M.A. 2003. Virtualness and knowledge in teams: Managing the love triangle of organizations, individuals, and information technology. *MIS Quarterly*, 27(2), 265–287.

Jarvenpaa, S.L. & Leidner, D.E. 1999. Communication and trust in global virtual teams. *Organization Science*, 10(6), 791–815.

Johnson, D.W. & Johnson, F.P. 1997. *Joining Together: Group Theory and Group Skills*, 6th ed. London: Allyn and Bacon.

Kirkman, B.L., Rosen, B., Tesluk, P.E. & Gibson, C.B. 2004. The impact of team empowerment on virtual team performance: The moderating role of face-to-face interaction. *Academy of Management Journal*, 47(2), 175–192.

Klitmoller, A. & Lauring, J. 2013. When global virtual teams share knowledge: Media richness, cultural difference and language commonality. *Journal of World Business*, 48(3), 398–406.

Nunamaker, J.F., Briggs, Jr., R.O., Mittleman, D.D. & Balthazard, P.B. 1998. Lessons from a dozen years of group support systems research: A discussion of lab and field findings. *Journal of Management Information Systems*, 13(3), 163–207.

Piccoli, G., Powell, A. & Ives, B. 2004. Virtual teams: Team control structure, work processes, and team effectiveness. *Information Technology and People*, 17, 359–379.

Solomon, C. 2012. The challenges of working in virtual teams: Virtual Teams Survey Report—2012. *RW Culture Wizard*. Retrieved January 27, 2016, available at http://rw-3.com/2012 VirtualTeamsSurveyReport.pdf.

Warkentin, M.E., Sayeed, L. & Hightower, R. 1997. Virtual teams versus face-to-face teams: An exploratory study of a Web-based conference system. *Decision Sciences*, 28(4), 975–996.

Yusof, S.A.M. & Zakaria, N. 2012. Exploring the state of discipline on the formation of swift trust within global virtual teams. *Proceedings of 45th Hawaii International Conference on System Sciences* (pp. 475–482). Maui, Hawaii. January 4–7, 2012.

Zakaria, N. & Yusof, S.A.M. 2015. Can we count on you at a distance? The impact of culture on formation of swift trust within global virtual teams. In J.L. Wildman & R.L. Griffith (Eds.), *Leading Global Teams* (pp. 253–268). New York: Springer.

Zigurs, I. 2003. Leadership in virtual teams: Oxymoron or opportunity? *Organizational Dynamics*, 31, 339–351.

Chapter 3

Characteristics and Elements of Global Virtual Teams

Introduction

Decades ago, teams relied on videoconferencing for meetings; nowadays, new collaborative communication technologies such as Trello, Skype, Google+, Zoom, and others have transformed the way people work at a distance. Moreover, the spread of social network tools like Facebook, WhatsApp, Twitter, and MySpace has made it much easier for teams to develop a relationship despite the lack of opportunities to meet physically. Thus, the effective management of globally distributed teams includes managing their virtual collaboration; this has become even more crucial as multinational corporations (MNCs) increase their reliance on the ability to transcend barriers of culture, distance, and time. In such a situation, culture does matter in the form of intercultural communication styles and the cultural values to which team members subscribe.

In global virtual teams (GVTs), although barriers such as time and space are reduced, communication barriers can be greater because of cultural differences. Not only are people geographically dispersed; they are also functionally diverse and bring in various areas of expertise, unique knowledge, and specialized skills (Morley et al. 2015). For example, a team composed of people from Malaysia, Canada, the United States, Britain, Germany, Japan, and France is more socially, culturally, and linguistically complex than a team composed of people from New York, Nebraska, Massachusetts, and California. The larger the cultural distance between GVT members, the greater the challenge of working together. Even for members that come from nearby geographical regions, for Eastern countries, the Japanese style of working is different from that of people from Thailand. The German negotiating style is different from the British. Hence, it is both demanding and complex to manage at a cultural level, but it is a necessity when GVT members may come from opposite ends of the world.

Given the two dimensions of time and space, studies in computer-supported cooperative work (CSCW) have developed a matrix illustrating the possible combinations (see Figure 3.1) and the possible working methods (Kirkman & Mathieu 2005; Johansen 1988). The two time dimensions are (1) *synchronous*—real-time communication that occurs at the same time and (2) *asynchronous*—communication occurs at different times (for example, I email you a question, and, a few hours later, you reply). The two place dimensions are (1) *same*—people meet in the same room, face to face and (2) *different*—people *meet* virtually while geographically distributed in multiple locations.

People in GVTs normally work autonomously and have inner-directed motivations. Yet they are also interdependent, need trust and commitment from others in the group, and share power and leadership based on individual members' technical and knowledge expertise. Members are bound by a common purpose, cooperative goals, and concrete measures

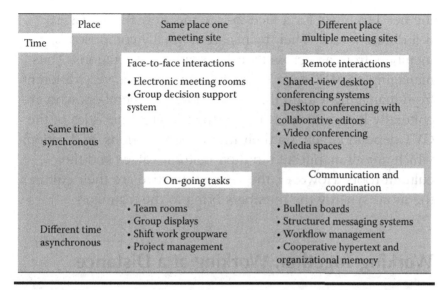

Place / Time	Same place one meeting site	Different place multiple meeting sites
Same time synchronous	**Face-to-face interactions** • Electronic meeting rooms • Group decision support system	**Remote interactions** • Shared-view desktop conferencing systems • Desktop conferencing with collaborative editors • Video conferencing • Media spaces
Different time asynchronous	**On-going tasks** • Team rooms • Group displays • Shift work groupware • Project management	**Communication and coordination** • Bulletin boards • Structured messaging systems • Workflow management • Cooperative hypertext and organizational memory

Figure 3.1 The time and space dimension for CSCW. (Adapted from Johansen R., *Groupware: Computer Support for Business Teams*, New York, The Free Press, 1988.)

of project effectiveness and the need to manage and coordinate their collaboration. These joint concerns become the basis for developing communication processes and norms, common rules for interacting, and a distinctive manner of thinking and behaving. The characteristics of a GVT can be divided into four aspects, each of which needs to be considered by MNCs when they embark on using this novel work structure.

Culturally Distinctive, Culturally Synergistic

GVTs are composed of *culturally heterogeneous* members. MNCs can no longer expect that their teams will contain only people of the same cultural orientations. Many local or regional companies, in an effort to cut their operating costs, initially introduced virtual teams to bring together people from different branches of the same organization. For example, marketing teams from different cities could communicate without the need to travel for a face-to-face meeting. For MNCs, it is a different case. Their teams are normally composed of members from all across their international operations. Thus, managing an MNC team's cultural complexity is very different from managing a team that is composed of members who are culturally homogeneous. The distinctive characteristics of the GVT depend largely on their mind-sets, emotions, and actions, which are all manifested in their cultural values and their cultural roots. However, the more distinctive are their cultures, the more synergy the members bring to the teamwork.

Working Together, Working at a Distance

GVT members will be *working together apart in* a geographically disperse environment. They will have few or no opportunities to meet their colleagues who may be thousands of miles away. They will rely heavily on computer-mediated communication (CMC) technologies, as well as social network systems. The biggest challenge of working in this environment is that members will need to learn to understand each other without any historical experience of each other's capability or past performance. Working together not only brings huge benefits such as the generation of ideas, the creation of innovative strategies, and strong collaboration, but it also builds skills in working together at a distance. Such work arrangements, without people meeting face to face, are no longer impossible. GVTs are a powerful strategy for recruiting the best human capital and leveraging their highest potential.

Technology Dependent, Technology Savvy

GVT members will *rely heavily on CMC* for their collaboration. Companies must therefore train their employees to be competent in using such technologies and to feel comfortable operating in a virtual environment. Technology continues to advance rapidly and exponentially, and GVT members need to keep abreast of new developments. Not only do they need to be competent culturally; they also need to be proficient technologically. It may be challenging to determine which and what types of software and technological applications to use. Team members can identify their preferences, but cultural values will influence such preferences. For example, Easterners who value nonverbal cues in their communication may prefer to use videoconferencing or Skype because, that way, they can see their colleagues' facial expressions when communicating. On the other hand, for Westerners, visual aspects of communication are secondary; they prefer to evaluate the explicit content of what other members communicate. They rely heavily on the textual content of conversations, rather than using emoticons (e.g., smiley faces), to convey their feelings or to infer the feelings of others.

Different Times, Different Urgency

Members will be operating in *different time zones*. This means that they need to align schedules in two or more countries when they plan their meetings. For example, when members from Singapore and America are working together, they need to accommodate the fact that they are 12 hours apart. The time dimension also has an underlying cultural aspect in that people view flexibility versus urgency differently. How and what people perceive about time, such as the degree of urgency to complete a task within a deadline, may vary based on culture. For example, some team members might need hours of deliberation and to weigh their options before finalizing a decision due to their habit of working in a hierarchical system, whereas, in other cultures, people can quickly make decisions because they feel empowered to do so, and they are held accountable for the decisions.

In conclusion, it is time for MNCs to engage in expert change management, strategic planning, global human resources management, and technology management in order to deploy GVTs in the most efficient and effective manner. Not only do these teams need to be trained in using various forms of collaborative technological tools; they also need to be prepared to cope with cultural diversity. On the one hand, technological tools can make high-performing teams more efficient and effective. On the other hand, it is more important to ensure that members are well coordinated in their assigned tasks, as well as compatible in their working styles, so that the challenges of working together at a distance can be minimized. In short, GVT collaboration not only requires people to work together but also demands the management of the participants' interdependent relationships as they work on common tasks, thus contributing toward common goals.

Case 3: Cultural Vignette

The Virtual Workplace: Working with Strangers in Cyberspace

In his inaugural meeting as a newly appointed CEO of Hewlett-Packard Tokyo, Mr. Bryan John announced that all managerial level executives would participate in global virtual teams effective next quarter—that is, next month. "We need to find ways to reduce our large operating costs," he explained. "One major expense is overseas assignments, which has both tangible costs such as travel and sending executives abroad as expatriates, and intangible costs such as the difficulty of adjusting to new cultures. Global virtual teams will enable us to work together at a distance, without leaving our home offices. With the sophisticated technology available today, I am confident that everyone is capable of working in this innovative teamwork structure." Following his announcement, he heard nothing: no cheers, no applause, and no salutes. Instead, he saw anxious, solemn, and grim faces across the room. There were a few minutes of total silence. He noticed some managers staring blankly at their colleagues, while others looked down with unhappy faces. Bryan was puzzled and surprised at receiving such a response. He had thought people would be delighted upon receiving such news, that they would be happy they would not need to go to the United States given the long and tiring hours of travel, and not forgetting the potentially painful adjustment period. In the corner, Mr. Namura Misoto tried to envision such a work platform and make sense of his manager's decision. Many questions rushed to his mind. He became anxious at the idea of facing such a drastic change. The good part, he thought, was that he wouldn't have to think about relocating. His unpleasant experience years ago as an expatriate in New York still haunted him. However, a lot of questions troubled his mind. "What is virtual teamwork? With whom will I work with—will they be strangers? How can I trust them? How will I communicate with them?" He thought about the normal greeting customs: bowing to a colleague when they met, offering courteous conversation, and only gradually engaging in discussion of work. Such customs were so ingrained in him that he feared it would be difficult to establish rapport with new team members if he could not observe their gestures, hear their tone of voice, and come to understand their way of working. He was also well aware of the direct style Americans were known for, and it intimidated him. In the virtual workspace, how could he deal with working with strangers in the absence of the many nonverbal

cues he was accustomed to rely on? He felt that
the change toward a global virtual team's structure
was coming too soon; they needed a longer time to
adjust. Silently, he opposed the decision. "I know
my people, I know the Japanese way of working!
We need cultural and technological training, so
they will feel competent and confident. Technology
is certainly prevalent in our workplace, but dealing
with human behavior, especially when combined
with cultural intricacies, is a serious challenge. Time
is essential."

References

Johansen, R. 1988. *Groupware: Computer Support for Business Teams*. New York: The Free Press.
Kirkman, B.L. & Mathieu, J.E. 2005. The dimensions and antecedents of team virtuality. *Journal of Management*, 31(5), 700–718.
Morley, S., Cormican, K. & Folan, P. 2015. An analysis of virtual team characteristics: A model for virtual project managers. *Journal of Technology Management & Innovation*, 10(1), 188–203.

CULTURE AND ITS MEANING

No argument, just keep it to oneself!

Promptly at 9 p.m., GMT Chief Financial Officer Mr. Andrew Tan began the virtual meeting. "Please explain to me what went wrong," he said. Mr. Chen offered a long explanation of what transpired between him and the supplier. Impatiently, Andrew said, "Our policy clearly states that all payments to suppliers need to be settled within no more than two weeks. We are dealing with an international supplier; you need to incorporate into your schedule the processing time for payment to be cleared." Indira Gomez and Peter Hosie, the marketing managers at the Australian branch, expressed their frustrations about the halted plans to launch their new product promotion in Vietnam that month. Other team members mentioned the repercussions of the delayed payment and bombarded Chen's finance team with questions. Overwhelmed and uncomfortable with confrontation, Chen decided to keep it simple and said, "I will make sure it gets settled ASAP," as he thinks to himself, "Whatever the problems are, there is no point in saying it outright. I don't want and I don't need to get into an argument."

Chapter 4

Overview of Culture and Cultural Values

Introduction

Edward Hall (1976), the founder of intercultural communication, asserted that "culture is communication and communication is culture" (p. 191). He emphasized that the types of information exchanged and shared, the reason a communication takes place, the way a person communicates, and to whom a person responds—all of these factors are rooted in the cultural values that a person subscribes to. What is meaningful to a person is based on how he or she perceives his or her world through the cultural lens that he or she holds and the cultural environment in which he or she lives.

Culture is an intricate concept with over 160 different definitions (Ferraro 2003; Schneider & Barsoux 1997; Kroeber & Kluckhohn 1952). One of the earliest and most widely cited definitions is "that complex whole which includes knowledge, belief, art, morals, law, custom, and any other capabilities and habits acquired by a man as a member of society" (Tylor 1871, p. 1). Ferraro (2001) defines culture as "everything that people have, think, and do as a member of their society" (p. 19).

In a similar vein, Hofstede (1980) sees culture as *software of the mind* or mental programming, analogous to the way that computers are programmed, composed of patterns of thinking, feeling, and acting. He sees culture as one of three layers of human mental programming, with specific components that differentiate it from the other two (see Figure 4.1).

The foundation layer is human nature, which Hofstede (1980) views as "what all human beings, from the Russian professor to the Australian aborigine, have in common: it represents the universal level in one's mental software. It is inherited with one's genes" (p. 5). Hooker (2003) places needs like food, shelter, and nurturing in this core set of commonalities that all human beings share. How one meets these needs, however, is derived from the other two layers. For example, all human beings need food; the difference lies in what people eat in different countries.

The second layer is culture. Culture is an intermediate layer between human nature and personality; it is cultivated, shared, and group based. Human beings learn from their experience and their surroundings; this, in turn, shapes their behaviors, attitudes, and values. All aspects of culture can be learned, taught, or observed from one's family, peers, or environment.

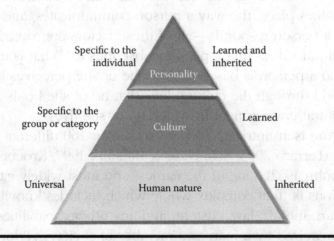

Figure 4.1   Three levels of human mental programming. (Hofstede, G., *Cultures and Organizations: Software of the Mind,* **New York: McGraw-Hill, 1991.)**

Culture can be studied from many perspectives (Karahanna et al. 2005; Kaarst-Brown & Evaristo 2002):

1. *National*—based on a person's country of origin.
2. *Ethnic*—based on shared background or descent; for example, Malaysia has three major ethnic groups: (1) Malay, (2) Chinese, and (3) Indian.
3. *Religious*—based on a shared set of spiritual beliefs, which may cross ethnic and national boundaries; for example, American or Arab Muslims and Chinese or Japanese Buddhists.
4. *Gender*—based on identification as female or male.
5. *Generational*—based on membership in an age cohort; for example, distinguishing grandparents from parents from children or elders from youngsters.
6. *Social*—based on educational background or professional status.
7. *Corporate or organizational*—based on work-related values arising from the way that people are socialized or oriented to the organization in which they work.
8. *Technological*—based on a shared technology, which can shape one's way of thinking, feeling, and acting; for example, norms inherent in technology usage or adoption.

Note that these different kinds of culture may overlap with, align with, or conflict with one another. For example, national culture may align with religious culture, corporate culture may conflict with gender culture, or technological culture may conflict with generational culture. A person may belong to many different types of culture over time, or to more than one at a time, depending on the situation.

The top layer of our *programming* is personality, which is unique to each individual human being. Personality is partly inherited, partly learned, and partly accumulated over the course of a person's life. In contrast to culture, personality is acquired over time, as well as inherited. Culture does influence a person's personality, since *acquired over time* equates to time spent immersed in a culture. Yet Hooker (2003) emphasizes that within a single culture, a wide range of personalities exists. It is thus misleading to use *national character* to stereotype all members of a country. For example, it is true to some extent that the Japanese emphasize politeness and tend to be reserved and introverted in nature, whereas Americans are often direct in their statements and possess extroverted personalities. However, there are also Japanese who are outspoken or rude and Americans who are shy or courteous.

In support of Hofstede's view of culture, Hall (1976) provides a more comprehensive analysis of the way culture touches our daily life:

> Culture is man's medium; there is not one aspect of human life that is not touched and altered by culture. This means personality, how people express themselves (including shows of emotion), the way they think, how they move, how problems are solved, how their cities are planned and laid out, how transportation systems function and are organized, as well as how economic and government systems are put together and function (pp. 16–17).

Despite the many variations of culture, anthropologists agree that culture has three distinct characteristics (Hall 1976):

1. *Culture is learned, not innate.* People learn how to behave, feel, or think according to what they experience in their social environment because culture is not derived from genetic characteristics.
2. *Culture is an interrelated complex whole.* Cultures are logical systems and provide coherent parts to a society.
3. *Culture is shared by a group or category and is not specific to an individual; rather, it is a collective concept.*

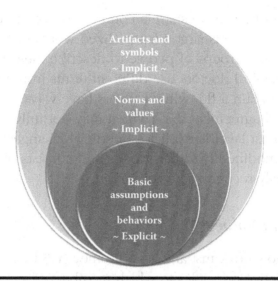

Figure 4.2   The onion model: Manifestations of culture at different levels. (Adapted from Hofstede G., *Cultures and Organizations: Software of the Mind,* **New York: McGraw-Hill, 1991; Schein E.H.,** *Organizational Culture and Leadership,* **1st ed., San Francisco: Jossey-Bass, 1985; Trompenaars F.,** *Riding the Waves of Culture— Understanding Diversity in Global Business,* **Chicago: Irwin, 1994.)**

Cultural Characteristics

Hofstede (1980) and Trompenaars (1994) suggested an *onion* model (see Figure 4.2) to describe the different layers of culture, with the degree of complexity increasing as one moves from the outer layers to the core. In the outermost layer is what people have or own, manifested as artifacts or material objects. In the middle layer is what a person thinks, reflected in their beliefs, attitudes, and values. Finally, in the innermost layer or core is what people do, determined or at least colored by their normative patterns of behaviors and assumptions.

Artifacts, Products, and Symbols

At the outermost layer of the onion are artifacts, products, or symbols, visible as gestures, words, images, or objects. People within the same culture share a common set of these symbols. One example is jargon (specialized words or language used by certain groups of people to describe their work). For example, medical doctors use different terms from the average person to explain a flu, while lawyers have ways of explaining a contractual agreement that laymen may not fully understand. This outermost layer is explicit, superficial, changeable, easily copied, or modified by other groups and consists of behaviors that are easily recognized or observed.

Norms and Values

According to Gudykunst and Ting-Toomey (1988, p. 61), norms are "prescriptive principles to which members of a culture subscribe." The underlying hypothesis of cultural value studies is that people from different cultures differ normatively in their value orientations, which ultimately results in differences in the overt behaviors that are exhibited by many of the people much of the time. Hofstede (1991) defines values as "a broad tendency to prefer certain states of affairs over others" (p. 8). Schwartz's (1992) definition is more elaborate, stating that values are "desirable states, objects, goals, or behaviors, transcending specific situations and applied as normative standards to judge and to choose among alternative modes of behavior" (p. 2). In support of this latter definition, Scarborough (1998) asserts that values are, in large part, culturally derived and, as a result, cultural values drive a person's beliefs, attitudes, and behaviors.

Basic Assumptions

Basic assumptions are the implicit or hidden aspects of culture that spring from needs at the core of human existence (Trompenaars 1994). Basic assumptions are the behavioral rules that regulate actions and guide people to workable ways of managing their relationships with the environment (external adaptation), as well as with other people (internal integration)

(Schneider & Barsoux 1997). At this core layer, behaviors often have unconscious motivations because basic assumptions are not articulated and are taken for granted. Several scholars have identified specific dimensions within this layer of culture: (a) Hall (1959, 1976) concerning time, space, and context; (b) Hofstede (1980) concerning work-related values; and (c) Trompenaars (1994) concerning business values. (See Chapter 6 for a more detailed discussion of these.) Hofstede's work on basic assumptions has enhanced our understanding of the complexities of culture, a vital perspective for organizations or people who need to work together to find solutions to shared problems.

References

Ferraro, G.P. 2003. *The Cultural Dimension of International Business*. Upper Saddle River, NJ: Prentice Hall.

Gudykunst, W.B. & Ting-Toomey, S. 1988. *Culture and Interpersonal Communication*. Newbury Park, CA: SAGE.

Hall, E.T. 1959. *Silent Language*. Garden City, NJ: Anchor Books/Doubleday.

Hall, E.T. 1976. *Beyond Culture*. Garden City, NJ: Anchor Books/Doubleday.

Hofstede, G. 1980. *Culture's Consequences: International Differences in Work-Related Values*. Beverly Hills, CA: SAGE Publications.

Hofstede, G. 1991. *Cultures and Organizations: Software of the Mind*. New York: McGraw-Hill.

Hooker, J. 2003. *Working Across Cultures*. Stanford, CA: Stanford Business Books.

Kaarst-Brown, M. & Evaristo, J.R. 2002. International cultures and insights into global electronic commerce. In P. Palvia, S. Palvia & E. Roche (Eds.), *Global Information Technology and Electronic Commerce*, 4th ed. (pp. 255–276). Marietta, GA: Ivey League Publishing.

Karahanna, E., Evaristo, J.R. & Strite, M. 2005. Levels of culture and individual behavior: An integrative perspective. *Journal of Global Information Management*, 13(2), 1–20.

Kroeber, A.L. & Kluckhohn, C. 1952. *Culture: A Critical Review of Concepts and Definitions*. Papers, 47 (1). Cambridge, MA: Peabody Museum of Archaeology and Ethnology.

Scarborough, J. 1998. *The Origins of Cultural Differences and Their Impacts on Management*. Westport, CT: Quorum Books.

Schein, E.H. 1985. *Organizational Culture and Leadership*, 1st ed. San Francisco: Jossey-Bass.

Schneider, S.C. & Barsoux, J. 1997. *Managing Across Cultures*. London: Prentice Hall.

Schwartz, S.H. 1992. Universals in the content and structure of values: Theory and empirical tests in 20 countries. In M. Zanna (Ed.), *Advances in Experimental Social Psychology* (Vol. 25, pp. 1–65). New York: Academic Press.

Trompenaars, F. 1994. *Riding the Waves of Culture—Understanding Diversity in Global Business*. Chicago: Irwin.

Tylor, E. 1871. *Origins of Culture*. New York: Harper & Row.

Chapter 5

Edward Hall: High-Context versus Low-Context Intercultural Communication

Introduction

As an anthropologist, Edward T. Hall (1976) examined the factors that influence intercultural understanding and thus enhance or impede communication between individuals from different cultural backgrounds. His work led him to formulate a cultural dimension called context. Context explains the way people evaluate and interpret the meaning of information that they receive. Hall stipulates that context comprises a system of meaning for information. It provides a model that enables people to comprehend communication forms ranging from the purely nonverbal (such as hand gestures, body language, facial expressions, and tone of voice) to the purely verbal (such as written text or spoken words).

Context is a continuous spectrum that reflects how much reliance a culture places on nonverbal cues in order to communicate: the heavier the reliance, the higher the context. Although context is a continuum, Hall focused on the two poles: (1) high context and (2) low context. Using context as a dichotomous variable highlights the differences in a more distinctive manner. Hall argues that, although people may use both high- and low-context communication, only one style is predominant at any given moment (Gudykunst et al. 1996).

Aside from context, Hall described several other dimensions that vary across cultures, for example, the meaning and importance of *time* and *space*. He focused on these two dimensions in his first book, *Silent Language* (1959), in which he observed variations between cultures not only in language but also in a communication phenomenon that goes beyond the use of language. This language of behavior, which he called *silent language*, constitutes elaborate prescriptions regarding how people handle time; spatial relationships; attitudes toward play, work, and learning; and more. Hall asserted that people frequently consider "time as an element of culture which communicates as powerfully as language" (p. 128), metaphorically known as *time talks*. The dimension of space, on the other hand, refers to the notion of a physical boundary that separates every living thing from its external environment, or, as he put it, *space speaks*.

In his later book, *Beyond Culture* (1976), Hall introduced the *context* dimension, another aspect of silent language. In this book, Hall focuses only on context, as it is the dimension with the strongest connection to communication. Context refers to the situational and informational aspects of message sharing; as Hall points out, the ability to glean shared meanings from nonverbal or paralinguistic cues affects communication between people from different cultural backgrounds. Language and the silent language are both critical in establishing common ground (Clark 1996). Obviously, then, communication challenges are amplified when people from different cultural values attempt to comprehend each other's indicators, signals, and nonverbal or verbal cues (Cassell & Tversky 2005; Pekerti & Thomas 2003).

According to Clark (1996), people establish common ground when they do something together, as a joint activity. When two people carry on a conversation, for example, several joint activities take place as they coordinate, manage, and synchronize their efforts to establish a mutual understanding, or common ground. Language is one of the many means that are used to establish common ground. This can be language in its most basic form, i.e., face to face (spoken), or in various kinds of written settings. The setting in which language is exchanged is known as the medium. In Clark's study, the medium is electronic and textual or written. Another important communicative element is *scene*, the place or situation in which the language is used.

Despite the fact that language is one of the most common bases for establishing common ground, it also can be a barrier in situations that rely on computer-mediated communication (CMC), such as email lists or blogs, since the vast majority of CMC is in English (Uljin et al. 2000; Cairncross 1997). Although English is known and used in the international business arena and is spoken with some degree of skill by many, it is not the first language for millions of people across the world. In addition, the slang terms used in one English-language culture may have obscure, opposite, or alternate meanings in another English-language environment. Interestingly, Ayyash-Abdo (2001) observed that the use of English might alter one's cultural orientation. Other studies have found that, when people use English in CMC, native and non-native English speakers exhibit differences in their discourse preferences and formats based on their cultural values (Uljin et al. 2000). Thus, participants collaborating via CMC need to be cognizant of and sensitive to English-language variations in style, format, tone, salutations, and closings, as these cues may affect the accuracy of their communication (Bloch & Starks 1999).

Milward (2000) further supports the theory that, although language matters, context can sometimes be more influential. Context influences what is being said, as well as when, where, to whom, and how. Thus, in Hall's framework, context refers to how much (and what kind of) information is required for the receipt and understanding of a message in a given communication situation. Victor (1992) discusses a behavior called *contexting,* which illustrates "the way in which one communicates and especially the circumstances surrounding that communication" (p. 137). Message senders need to take the culturally normative communication context into account when they formulate a message, and, to varying degrees, message receivers must also interpret the message using unique cues that are obtained from the communication context (Zakaria et al. 2003).

As Peter Ehrenhaus says,

> [M]embers of cultures where high-context messages predominate are sensitive to situational features and explanations, and tend to attribute others' behavior to the context, situation, or other factors external to the individual. Members of cultures in which low-context messages predominate, in contrast, are sensitive to dispositional characteristics and tend to attribute others' behavior to characteristics internal to the individual (e.g., personality). Individuals use the information that they believe is important when interacting with members of other cultures. (Triandis 1994, p. 127)

Hall's contextual dimension helps predict how high-context individuals will internalize the meaning of information based on nonverbal elements—they rely more on the context and less on the content. Low-context individuals, on the other hand, are concerned with the content of the information, such as the explicit words and the message itself, and put less emphasis on the context. Simply put, Hall's contextual

Table 5.1 Summary of High- and Low-Context Cultures

Component	High Context	Low Context
Cultural understanding	Requires an adequate understanding of a particular culture in order to function well within the society.	Requires little knowledge of culture to get along, and culture does not play an important role in forming individual identity.
Cultural assumptions	Assumes a rich common culture, and the identity of individual members is defined in terms of that culture.	Does not assume a common culture. A member of another society can function well by simply adhering to minimal legal restrictions.
Nature of information	Information is implicit and requires little background or explanations since people are assumed to have prior knowledge.	Information is made explicit in each interaction, where everything is spelled out clearly.
Information cues	Important information is transmitted through nonverbal and contextual cues.	Important information is transmitted through explicit verbal messages.
Speech and style of communication	Speech and communication are indirect, and ambiguous language is common; people tend to avoid saying *no* directly.	Speech and communication are direct and straight to the point; people value verbal and eloquent speech and tend to express opinions and intentions freely and directly persuade others to accept their viewpoints.

(Continued)

Table 5.1 (Continued)   Summary of High- and Low-Context Cultures

Component	High Context	Low Context
Background knowledge	Have a wide network of sources and stay well informed on many subjects.	Verbalize more background information and tend not to be well informed on subjects outside of their own specialties or interests.
Cultural action–orientation	Prioritize the establishment of relationships over the achievement of goals. The emphasis is on relationship; relationship oriented.	Prioritize accomplishment of objectives and goals over relationships. The emphasis is on the goal; task oriented.
Cultural expressiveness	Feelings and thoughts not openly expressed. Often, messages must be read between the lines.	Feelings and thoughts often explicitly expressed, verbally or in written. People value being *true to their feelings*.
Cultural distinctions between working and personal relationships	All aspects of an individual's life permeate and connect to everything else in his or her life.	Personal, work, and other relationships are highly compartmentalized, with little overlap.
Background experiences	People are homogeneous, with extensive shared experiences, information, and networks.	People have independent experiences, information, and networks, which may vary drastically.

Source: Zakaria, N. et al., *Information Technology & People,* 16, 49–75, 2003.

dimension reflects the ways in which individuals perceive, exchange, use, and communicate information. All cultures, whether high or low context, have their own unique identity, language, nonverbal communication cues, material culture, history, and social structures. In essence, Hall views culture as a system for creating, sending, storing, and processing information (Hall & Hall 1990), and his work is summarized in Table 5.1.

References

Ayyash-Abdo, H. 2001. Individualism and collectivism: The case of Lebanon. *Social Behaviors and Personality*, 29(5), 503–518.

Bloch, B. & Starks, D. 1999. The many facets of English: Intra-language variation and its implications for international business. *Corporate Communications*, 4, 80–88.

Cairncross, F. 1997. *The Death of Distance: How the Communications Revolution Will Change Our Lives*. Boston: Harvard Business School Press.

Cassell, J. & Tversky, D. 2005. The language of online intercultural community formation. *Journal of Computer-Mediated Communication*, 10(2), article 2. Retrieved August 23, 2005, available at http://jcmc.indiana.edu/vol10/issue2/cassell.html.

Clark, H.H. 1996. *Using Language*. Cambridge, MA: Cambridge University Press.

Hall, E.T. 1959. *Silent Language*. Garden City, NJ: Anchor Books/Doubleday.

Hall, E.T. 1976. *Beyond Culture*. Garden City, NJ: Anchor Books/Doubleday.

Hall, E.T. & Hall, M.R. 1990. *Understanding Cultural Differences: Germans, French and Americans*. Boston: Intercultural Press, Inc.

Gudykunst, W.B., Matsumoto, Y., Ting-Toomey, S., Nishida, T., Kim, K. & Heyman, S. 1996. The influence of cultural individualism-collectivism, self-construal, and individual values on communication styles across cultures. *Human Communication Research*, 22(4), 510–543.

Milward, S. 2000. The relationship among Internet exposure, communicator context and rurality. *American Communication Journal*, 3(3). Retrieved September 20, 2005, available at http://www.acjournal.org/holdings/vol3/Iss3/rogue4/milward.

Pekerti, A.A. & Thomas, D.C. 2003. Communication in intercultural interaction: An empirical investigation of idiocentric and sociocentric communication styles. *Journal of Cross-Cultural Psychology*, 34(2), 139–154.

Uljin, J., O'Hair, D., Weggeman, M., Ledlow, G. & Hall, H.T. 2000. Innovation, corporate strategy, and cultural context: What is the mission for international business communication? *The Journal of Business Communication*, 37, 293–316.

Triandis, H.C. 1994. *Culture and Social Behavior*. New York: McGraw-Hill.

Victor, D.A. 1992. *International Business Communication*. New York: HarperCollins.

Zakaria, N., Stanton, J.M. & Sarkar-Barney, S.T.M. 2003. Designing and implementing culturally-sensitive IT applications: The interaction of culture values and privacy issues in the Middle East. *Information Technology & People*, 16, 49–75.

Chapter 6

Fons Trompenaars and Charles Hampden-Turner: Seven Cultural Dimensions: A Mirror Image of Problem-Solving in the Workplace

Introduction

In the late 1980s, Fons Trompenaars emerged as a respected theorist who contributed complementary cultural dimensions to the field of cross-cultural management. Together with Charles Hampden-Turner, he established a consultation firm called the Centre for International Business Studies, and, since then, they have worked with numerous leading multi-national corporations (MNCs) including British Petroleum, Philips, IBM, Heineken, AMD, Mars, Motorola, General Motors, Merrill Lynch, Johnson & Johnson, Pfizer, ABN AMRO, ING, PepsiCo, and Honeywell. They have also conducted more than a thousand cross-cultural training programs in 20 countries. In late 1990s, due to his wide-ranging consultation work, Trompenaars was ranked as one of the top management consultants, among other gurus like Tom Peters, Edward de Bono, Michael Porter, and Peter Drucker. He developed his understanding of cultural influences on organizations based on his years of consultation and practice rather than on scholarly work, contrary to other cross-cultural theorists like Hofstede, Hall, Kluckhorn, and Strodtbeck. Between 2011 and 2013, he became one of the top 20 most influential thinkers in human resources management and enlightened scholars on many aspects of culture and its influence in the workplace. His inquisitive mind explored how people's approaches to solving problems at work are shaped and influenced by their own cultural values and why people from different cultures see the world differently, rooted in a dynamic cultural values orientation.

Trompenaars (1994) recognized that people act in response to the way that they naturally see and perceive the world. How one sees the world defines how one's problem-solving mind develops. Our perceptions can sometimes result in a dilemma when we are confronted with choices or a range of paths to take when solving a problem. Oftentimes, managers faced with this dilemma are challenged to function at a higher level of cognitive and emotional competency. Trompenaars poses thought-provoking questions and seeks answers in different ways, supporting his work with wide-ranging justifications. He found many of the answers through the MNCs that he had worked with over the years. Some of his explanations are built upon the work of previous cross-cultural theorists, but his approach to and views about culture differ slightly from those of other theorists because the organizations he had worked with are highly diverse, both in the field of business and in size. Whereas Hofstede's research was based on a survey sent to only one organization (IBM employees), and Hall interviewed people during his involvement with a single organization (the Foreign Service Institute), Trompenaars' research was based on his consultation work with many different organizations.

What concerns Trompenaars and Hampden-Turner is that it takes time for people from different cultures to uncover the similarities and dissimilarities in values, practices, and attitudes. People may also find it difficult to tolerate and accept these dissimilarities because cultural values operate at the group/societal level rather than at the individual level—i.e., the level of a single person's personality (refer to the *triangle* cultural model in Chapter 4). On the one hand, such group-based values may change over time as they are fluid, not rigid. On the other hand, culture is sustainable in a society over a prolonged period of time due to the inherited values and customary practices and therefore may take time to change. In organizations, people who work together may, over time, develop common routines, procedures, and practices for carrying out a task, which are influenced by the cultural values belonging to the society. For example, in the early 1980s, a manager at the headquarters of an MNC might send a fax to a subordinate in another department. Fax was an accepted communication mode. Although this was a common practice, in certain cultures, including many Asian ones, faxes are not well accepted (Chen 2006). In a collectivistic society, people still prefer to pick up the phone to communicate because the nonverbal cues present in one's voice are more meaningful than purely textual communication, which strips out these nonverbal cues.

When information technology was introduced into the workplace, the fax machine was replaced by email for urgent exchanges or for messages to be delivered to a branch across the country. Again, some cultures resisted email as a communication mode due to the absence of nonverbal cues (Sproull & Kiesler 1996). Nowadays, more and more organizations and people are shifting to different communication platforms. People are more comfortable with social network sites such as

Facebook, Twitter, WhatsApp, and other newly emergent communication and collaboration tools and platforms, which make sending emails seem antiquated. As time goes by, technology becomes more and more sophisticated, making cross-cultural communication around the globe faster and cheaper. People respond to these new tools with innovation, developing more efficient ways of doing things. Past practices become obsolete resulting in changes to a society's culture, and thus new cultures evolve in organizations. However, there are certain aspects of the workplace that are difficult to change—for example, shifting the organizational structure from a tall and hierarchical system to a flatter, more empowerment-based system. In certain cultures, it can take much longer to shift from a bureaucratic system to an empowered system, depending on how swiftly those involved in decision making are willing to accept and adapt.

In essence, Trompenaars and Hampden-Turner see workplace dilemmas and problems as a mirror image of individual behaviors. Why so? Their views were based on one clear idea, "Culture is the way in which a group of people solves problems and reconciles dilemmas" (Trompenaars & Hampden-Turner 1998, p. 6). The symbol of a mirror refers to the idea that every single problem that is rooted at the cultural level is actually a reflection of oneself against others. Each society has its own world view, its own ideas about how things are to be done, while others may have a completely opposite outlook. Thus, a society needs to explore and be aware of other world views so that it can evaluate culture-related circumstances and situations realistically.

Human behaviors in the workplace can be analyzed based on three orientations, abbreviated as PET: (1) *people*—the relationship of people to people, (2) *environment*—the relationship of people to the control of the internal and external environment, and (3) *time*—the relationship of people to time. These three orientations are derived from two things: first, how human beings deal with each other and why they behave in a certain way, and, second, how such behaviors are linked to people's cultural values. Using this cultural framework, there are two ways to understand the influence of culture on decision making in global virtual teams (GVTs): first, how an individual can get to know himself or herself at a deeper level and find ways to relate to others, and, second, how managers can better understand others when managing a multicultural team. Within the PET cultural framework, Trompenaars identified seven dimensions, each of which represents a two-sided problem-solving characteristic: (1) universalism versus particularism, (2) individualism versus communitarianism, (3) neutral versus emotional, (4) specific versus diffuse, (5) achievement versus ascription, (6) internal versus external control, and (7) sequential versus synchronic. The following paragraphs describe these seven dimensions and demonstrates how the three orientations can be applied as a theoretical lens, specifically in the context of GVTs and how culture affects the decision-making process.

People Orientation (P)

People find it challenging to understand and fully accept cultural differences unless they are sufficiently culturally aware and educated to be able to celebrate the similarities that they share as human beings. Trompenaars identified five work orientations, defined as how people deal with others in a work environment, which any manager should clearly understand.

First, the manager must balance abiding by rules with maintaining relationships. Universalism holds that rules and procedures are there to be followed and that things are to be done accordingly to policy—this is associated with task orientation. Particularism emphasizes the need for building rapport and close connections with others and a sensitivity to how and why individuals can be affected differently by the same rules—this is associated with relationship orientation. This balancing act is complex because it creates a dilemma regarding whether a workplace issue can be solved through policies and guidelines or whether it requires strong bonding and relationships that are established over time.

Second, the manager must be aware of individualistic versus collectivistic values as practiced in the workplace, whether his or her people are doing things based on a self-driven goal, in which *I* and *myself* are the drivers, or a group-driven goal, which prioritizes *we* and *ourselves* and promotes collective efforts. In some cultures, the word we illustrates the importance of working together and cherishes and inculcates team spirit. However, an individualistic culture prioritizes I and self-rewarding accomplishments; to meet this need for self-control and independence requires managers to foster an environment of empowerment. Individualistic versus collectivistic values may also affect how people view the decision-making process. In a team context, team members from individualistic cultures may use a *self-opinionated* voice when engaging in discussions, thereby promoting a healthy exchange of ideas and creating synergy; they do not see this as threatening in a team brainstorming session. By contrast, individuals from a collectivistic culture may be hesitant to voice their feelings for fear that it will create animosity in others. They may prefer to keep their feelings to themselves until they are required to voice an opinion—which they then do in a safe and nonconfrontational manner, since what matters most to this culture is the display of a *collective mind* within the team, without bold displays of contradictory opinions.

Third, managers need to understand how people display their emotions, whether they favor a nondisclosing, nonconfrontational manner—a neutral way of expressing feelings—or whether they tend to be expressive and emotional, openly speaking of their anger, excitement, or joy. This dimension is an important aspect of culture because people communicate their feelings in two ways: (1) verbal and (2) nonverbal. In a culture that is neutral in nature, people are more comfortable displaying their emotions through nonverbal means, such as facial expressions, hand gestures, body movements, the use of silence, and so on. However, in cultures that are expressive, people will normally employ clear and explicit verbal and written methods to communicate their opinions, though they may use nonverbal cues to support their arguments. They will state their emotions without reservation.

Fourth, managers need to understand how people define the boundary between their personal and working lives. The specific versus diffuse dimension addresses this question. On the specific end of the spectrum, people make a clear division between work and play; in such a culture, people maintain a logical separation between work inside the office and fun outside the office. In other words, the work boundary is not blurred by their private lives. For a culture that is diffuse, on the other hand, work and play can overlap. This overlap occurs due to the strong relationships that people in such cultures strive to develop, protect, and maintain over time.

The fifth and last dimension is achievement versus ascription, the question of *who did what* versus *who knows whom*. We often think that status in the workplace should be based purely on individual accomplishments, i.e., what one can offer and what one can contribute. At the end of the day, what counts most are objective outcomes and deliverables that are shown in the form of productivity. Cultures with this mind-set are known as achievement cultures. By contrast, in an ascription culture, people are evaluated based on who they are and whom they are affiliated with. Status is based on unwritten rules, and the real goal may not be measurable achievements but rather how one can influence others. Managers need to learn how their people perceive and award status.

Environment Orientation (E)

PET's environment orientation refers to the locus of control, either internal or external. The key questions are how people

control their environment and whether people believe that a
problem originates from an external versus an internal source.
Do we control our environment, or are we controlled by it?
Do we control nature or let it take its course? In an organizational context, the answers to these questions are crucial when
people need to make decisions, whether major or minor.

Managers may face a situation in which decisions are outside their control due to a bureaucratic system in which power
is concentrated at the top management level, moves down to
the middle level, and then finally to lower management. Such
multilayered formality is often found in Asian countries. These
cultures have an external locus of control in that team members are not empowered to make individual decisions. Instead,
decisions are made either by a collective voice based on consensus or, if a single voice, that of the person with the highest
authority in the company. In a culture based on an internal
locus of control, by contrast, each person can act individually; he or she is given responsibility and empowered to make
decisions. For managers, the environment orientation is significant in understanding the degree of power that people feel
that they have in the decision-making process, as well as what
drives or motivates them.

For example, consider the internal control dimension.
Trompenaars explains that people with an internal locus
are naturally self-driven and believe that they *own* all their
decisions—that is, that they will be held accountable for their
actions and outcomes. On the other hand, those with an external locus of control feel that things ought to remain in com-
pliance with the current environment and that they have no
real power to change how things are done; they rely on their
superiors to make the best decisions or depend on a group
of people coming to an agreement together. External-locus
people feel that decisions do not rest in their own hands but
in those of others—either in a collective effort by the team or
in a superior power, i.e., their boss—whereas internal-locus
people believe that achievement is obtained through self-effort

and that one can freely plan, organize, and execute different outcomes with little or no reference to others.

Time Orientation (T)

What is the nature of time, and how do people perceive and manage time in the workplace? According to Ferraro (2010), "in some respects, time speaks more plainly than words, for time conveys powerful messages about how people relate to the world and each other" (p. 125). Trompenaars draws a clear distinction between cultures with a sequential time dimension versus those with a synchronic time dimension, by asking the question, "Do people do things one at a time (sequentially) or several things at once (synchronically)?" Applied to the work context, this dichotomy describes whether team members stick to the agenda during meetings and carry out tasks in a sequential and systematic manner, or juggle many things at one time, wherein all tasks are woven into subtasks. In the former case, team members may be inflexible and unwilling to adjust schedules; in the latter case, they may lose track of time, wander off topic, be less punctual when attending meetings, or miss assigned due dates.

Managers need a good understanding of their team members' time orientation because different people have different senses of time and different approaches to time management. Trompenaars and Hampden-Turner (1998) looked at time management as a set of activities that are planned, organized, and implemented based on either sequentially or synchronically oriented decisions. They asserted that "time can be legitimately conceived of as a line of sequential events passing us at regular intervals. It can also be conceived of as cyclical and repetitive, compressing past, present and future by what these have in common: seasons and rhythms" (p. 126). Time is not only defined physically, according to the numbers on a clock, but also has a deeper level. Time can refer to the physical aspect of how a person values the ticking of a clock, and, of course, when people talk about deadlines, the only kind of time that matters is clock time, first in the form of minutes and hours and then extended to days, weeks, months, and even years. Yet time can also be interpreted from a psychological standpoint in terms of the sense of urgency that a person feels regarding tasks to be completed—either a precise and punctual time or a *loose reckoning*, as suggested by Ferraro and Brody (2012). Several other theorists have explored time-distinctive values, including Edward Hall's (1976) monochronic (M-time) versus polychronic (P-time), and Walker and Walker's (1995) concept of single focus versus multifocus.

All these theorists share the same underlying goal, which is to understand how people perceive time and how they manage time at work. Trompenaars and Hampden-Turner (1998) took their work a step further, exploring how managers can better understand the relationship between time orientation and human relations. People with a synchronic time orientation appreciate relationships with other people, and such ties are considered valuable; past, present, and future are interrelated to the extent that a historical relationship is seen as important for both current conditions and future projects since it creates strong bonds of warmth. In synchronic time orientation, a relationship takes precedence over a task, even though relationships need to be developed, and that process is time consuming. Since they feel that time can wait, they value taking things slowly and see no need to rush in delivering a task; as a result, tasks may be put off. For example,

> [Imagine that] A person is attending to his new cus-
> tomer at a counter. Then, a phone rings, he picks
> up the phone, and, with pleasure, he welcomes the
> customer on the other line because she is his favor-
> ite and regular customer. Due to his long-established

relationship with the old customer, he needs to
spend time to entertain her. Thus, the new customer
needs to wait. Then, his clerk comes to his desk to
ask him to sign a document, and, again, he has to
stop talking to his old customer while signing the
document, and the new customer has to wait further.

On the other end of the spectrum, sequential time orientation views relationships as instrumental and maintains a clear
boundary between ties and tasks; this separation between
time intervals underlines the separation between means and
ends. Interpersonal relationships are formed with a clear
objective in mind to achieve a desired outcome. Yet relationships cannot be sacrificed to accomplish a goal. Normally,
task completion for a team is not dependent on the degree
or strength of the relationships among its members. Each task
has its own process, and the process follows a systematic path
from point A to point B. Each task has a timeline and specific objectives. Task takes priority over relationships. Time
is money, and, therefore, time is a tangible commodity that
needs to be used to the optimum and maximum. Tasks are
assigned, and people are expected to meet deadlines, establish
milestones, and organize schedules in line with the project
objectives.

Conclusion

Trompenaars and Hampden-Turner (1998) successfully applied
their theoretical lens to offer enlightening and insightful suggestions as to how managers at MNCs can prepare themselves
to deal with problems in the workplace arising from cultural
differences. What is important to recognize is that work-related
problems are rooted in our cultural values, and our ways of
thinking and feeling, which are manifested in our behaviors.

References

Chen, G.M. 2006. Asian communication studies: What and where to now. *The Review of Communication*, 6(4), 295–311.

Ferraro, G. & Brody, E.K. 2012. *Cultural Dimension of Global Business*. New York: Routledge.

Ferraro, G.P. 2010. *The Cultural Dimension of International Business*. Upper Saddle River, NJ: Prentice Hall.

Hall, E.T. 1976. *Beyond Culture*. Garden City, NJ: Anchor Books/ Doubleday.

Sproull, L.S. & Kiesler, S. 1986. Reducing social context cues: Electronic mail in organizational communication, management. *Science*, 32, 1492–1512.

Trompenaars, F. 1994. *Riding the Waves of Culture—Understanding Diversity in Global Business*. Chicago: McGraw-Hill.

Trompenaars, F. & Hampden-Turner, C. 1998. *Riding the Waves of Culture: Understanding Diversity in Global Business*. New York: McGraw-Hill.

Walker, B.T.D. & Walker, T. 1995. *Doing Business Internationally: The Guide to Cross-Cultural Success*. New York: Irwin.

DISTRIBUTED DECISION-MAKING PROCESSES AND ACTIVITIES

What can I do, it is the bureaucracy!

Henry Butler, the marketing manager at Sime Tyres in London, waited and waited for a decision. He looked at the calendar. He was frustrated because they were behind the deadline for almost one week now. He should receive the final say from the team in Thailand and then communicate it to their Swiss team. The meeting will be held in Geneva, and it is just around the corner. Without waiting any further, he decided to send a quick email—"Prawan, what is your decision? Who will be the speaker and how many participants?" The Swiss team member, Anthony Marcus, as the project manager of Alphard Consulting Inc., was shocked that the awaited decision has not been made by Prawan because he needs to organize and coordinate the event with Henry. He was also getting anxious about it and thus decided to respond to the email, which said "...we are running short of time, we need to finalize the number of people to attend the meeting. It is only three weeks away. Please get back to us promptly." Henry and Anthony are still waiting despite the two emails that were sent. Time is ticking, yet decisions were not made. In his bewilderment, Anthony wonders, "...hmmm, how do I push the team to make decisions urgently?" While on the other corner of the world, Henry sighed and said to himself, "If only they are in my office, I will surely knock on their doors. Unfortunately, they are thousands of miles away!"

Chapter 7

Overview of Distributed Decision-Making Process

Introduction

Who makes the decision? What kinds of decisions do people make at the workplace, and for what reasons are they carried out, and when are they needed? If at all, can one transfer or empower the responsibility of making decisions to others? To answer these questions, let me first define what decision making is. According to Saaty (2012), making decisions in organizations undergoes a multifaceted process based on many intricate and challenging issues, despite the fact that people need to make decisions at all times and at all levels. He further suggests that decision making is a complex world, and it is governed by two dimensions, which are the human behavioral and thought process. The human behaviors are driven by the instinct–drive theory, which describes how a person is subjected to one's own instinct when making decisions. As such, factors like sentiment, value, ambition, attitude, taste and preferences, and inclination are seen as more desirable compared to logic reasoning and logic thinking. Saaty (2012) also further integrates the theory of learning to understand how a person makes a decision. He defined learning as "...the ability to recognize a specific act in the light of previous experience. It is an iterative, or repeated, process of adding knowledge that elaborates on or expands existing knowledge" (p. 9). With both theories at hand, it is interesting to explore whether or not such intuitive and learning behaviors of people at the workplace provide an understanding on how the different work structures, such as the virtual work environment, play out when it comes to the decision-making process.

Essentially, given the heightened level of globalization and the ubiquitous use of computer-mediated technologies in organizations at present, people are confronted with new ways of making decisions at a virtual workplace. Thus, with this entire complex distributed decision-making process, it is essential to understand that the decision-making process is still the root of management roles in any organizations. In a globalized world, the reality of workplace presents each employee at multiple layers of management with varied types of decisions for diverse reasons at a different time zone with different practices as well. In fact, in all organizations, all layers of management are involved in decision making— i.e., one way or another—whether or not it is for a simple or challenging task at the workplace. For example, on a daily and routine basis, no organization can operate without making decisions—either small or big ones. The only difference that sets apart one layer of management from the others is the degree of decisions to be made, by whom, and by when. Likewise, on a long-term and competitive basis, no organization can excel without making timely and accurate decisions within a strategic time frame. If organizations regard time as money, then decisions are costly. High-performing organizations depend on efficient decisions and effective action plans. The phrase *money talks* becomes the main agenda for any organization to incorporate its strategic plan of maximizing profits and minimizing costs. The goal of making profit is the bottom line for all organizations.

Many organizations consider the decision-making process as the heart of organizational process, culture, and structure; thus, for the distributed decision-making process to be effective, organizations need to consider such process as both a science and art in itself. Moreover, for global virtual teams (GVTs), given the complexities of distance and time zone, decisions need to carefully incorporate the scientific process because, in every step of a decision, people need to explore situations and problems, then identify the choices when they need to solve a problem, consequently think carefully about the problems and the choices at hand, deliberate the ideas among people, and finally arrive at a solution by taking appropriate actions. It is in a scientific manner because it follows a systematic way of doing things—involving one process to another, which has *a beginning* and *an end*. This process itself can be time consuming because the members are from different geographical locations with different time zones. Yet, GVTs are also confronted with many challenges in arriving to a decision, as well as realizing an action due to cultural differences such as in communication styles, work practices, and procedures. This is where the *aesthetic* or creativity element comes into the picture. The art of decision making entails a manager to solve a problem and find a solution through an innovative way by taking the cultural elements into perspective. It may result in diverse ways of solving a problem to reach efficient and effective decisions. People, organization system and structures, work policies and procedures, and technology are some of the key aspects that need to be put in place at the organizational level. Yet many of the organizations failed to take into consideration the magnitude and impact of the *virtual-space* factors when they manage their GVTs due to members coming from different organizations. They failed to incorporate both the scientific and innovative manner of managing the distributed decision-making process.

Therefore, this study focused on email participation and did not consider other computer-mediated communication

(CMC) tools such as blogs or Wiki Webs, or Web conferencing, or face-to-face meetings. Effective participation in the World Summit on the Information Society (WSIS) was measured by the substantive contributions that were made by Civil Society participants during the four stages of the decision-making process: (1) problem recognition/agenda setting, (2) information search, (3) specification of alternatives, and (4) choice. I investigated the communicative behaviors from two distinct cultural orientations, high context and low context, since an individual may contribute in the four stages differently depending on whether he or she uses high-context versus low-context cultural communication styles and the cultural values that one is ascribed to.

The first stage in decision making is problem recognition (Adler 1997). It was crucial for participants to correctly identify and recognize the problems that they wanted to solve or bring to attention in the WSIS. This is the initial step in the decision-making process. In public policy-making processes, Kingdon (1995) termed this stage as *agenda setting*. The second stage is a response to problems and issues, which Adler termed as information search. At this stage, once people identify the problems, as well as begin to look for ways to solve them, they would provide many responses as a way to search for information that helps them make a decision on the most viable solution for the problem encountered (Adler 1997). The third stage is specification of alternatives in which people choose from a range of options (Kingdon 1995). In this stage, it centers on the ability of a Civil Society participant to make a proposal by giving or generating ideas, and presenting a position on the problems identified, or putting across self-interest issues. The final stage is called *choice* where a solution (one or many or even a nonsolution) is arrived at either by consensus or by authoritative action. It is noteworthy that success in one of these stages is not an indication of success in others. In addition, the stages do not necessarily occur in a linear fashion. The stages are iterative and interdependent and may occur several times before a solution is reached and/or agreed upon by participants. Likewise, some stages can be left out. The most *effective* process is that participants reach a solution that addresses the problem and that arises from the proposals made and the responses generated.

In phase one of the WSIS in Geneva, the outcome was to generate two documents—(1) Declaration of Principles and (2) Plan of Action. However, this study did not look at the impact of culture on the WSIS *outcome* but rather focused on the *process*—the effect of culture on the dynamics of Civil Society participants' cultural communicative behaviors using email (as pointed out in the circle area of Figure 7.1). The decision-making processes are only based among and within Civil Society participants and not on the overall WSIS processes that include the other two multistakeholders—(1) governments and (2) private sectors.

Initially, this study identified four stages based on Kingdon's (1995) and Adler's (1997) models. In a virtual work structure,

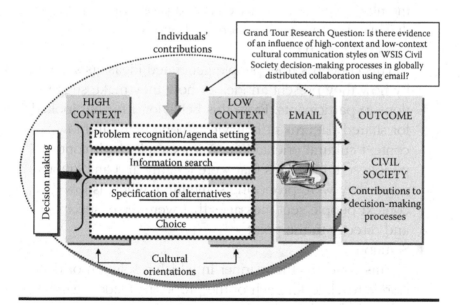

Figure 7.1   Conceptual framework of globally distributed collaboration of Civil Society in WSIS using email.

the decision-making process will be amplified by several more factors. Distance, space, technology, and culture will pose challenges for managers to make decisions. Thus, by analyzing the data empirically, the stages of decision-making process were reduced to only three. The stage called responses and deliberation was integrated with the other three main stages because it was observed that participants continuously provided responses that became a cyclical feedback that fed into the three key stages. Thus, the stage called *responses and deliberation* was no longer considered one stage by itself. In this study, I defined effective participation based on two criteria: (1) *quantity*—number of emails and frequency and (2) *quality*—substance of emails.

■ Problem identification

This concerns messages in which participants identified a problem(s) or an issue(s). Some of the issues were in a form of question, while some were in a form of statement. This activity is crucial as it sets the initial tone for member participation; a well-stated problem is more easily solved than a poorly identified one.

■ Proposal making

This concerns how people generated ideas, as shown by how they present an idea or how they make suggestions to participants. From this behavior, I further looked for shared patterns of behavior among high- and low-context cultural orientations. For example, high-context people sent messages that were lengthy and ambiguous when they were proposing something, whereas low-context people sent messages that were terse, succinct, and directly to the point.

■ Solution

This concerns the manner in which a solution or decision is reached for each of the proposals made, again from a cultural standpoint. Each solution was considered a decision point. For this analysis, I looked only at proposals that had a decision. If the proposal did not have a decision point, I regarded it as an instance without a decision or solution.

Theoretical Models of Decision-Making Process

In exploring the impact of culture on decision-making processes, I used a combination of two theoretical frameworks: (1) cultural contingencies of decision making (Adler 1997) and (2) public policy-making processes (Kingdon 1995). Adler proposes five sequential steps in decision making that have cultural consequences: (1) problem recognition, (2) information search, (3) construction of alternatives, (4) choice, and (5) implementation. Kingdon's (1995) model identifies four steps: (1) agenda setting, (2) specification of alternatives, (3) choice among specified alternatives, and (4) implementation.

This framework is useful in understanding the policy-making processes in WSIS Geneva, beginning from the time that the listserv members identify a problem or an issue to the time that they reach a solution. Although Adler's model has five stages, and Kingdon's model has four, both describe a similar sequence of actions. Adler underlines decision-making processes as a crucial managerial task that is culturally bound (see Figure 7.2), whereas Kingdon's model explicates the policy-making processes. It is useful to note that in Adler's model, steps 2 and 3 can be collapsed to correspond with Kingdon's step 2, thus enabling me to use both models. For the purposes of this study, I chose to model out the decision-making processes based on the synthesis of Adler's first four stages and Kingdon's first three stages and the final stage—implementation—is omitted (see Figures 7.1 and 7.2).

Based on Figure 7.2, the first step is problem recognition/agenda setting. Adler introduced the stage called problem recognition in which members identify and define the problem that they are facing and recognize the severity of the

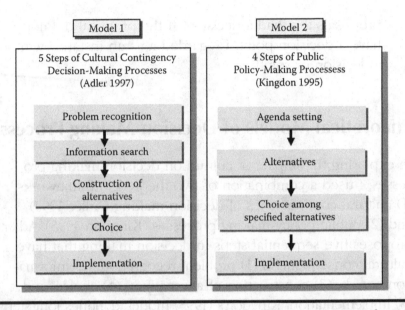

Figure 7.2   Sequential models of decision-making processes. (Adapted from Kingdon, J.W., *Agendas, Alternatives, and Public Policies***, New York, Addison-Wesley Longman, 1995; Adler, N.J.,** *International Dimensions of Organizational Behavior***, 3rd. ed., Cincinnati, OH, South-Western, 1997.)**

problem. According to Adler (1997), it is imperative to recognize "when is a problem a problem" (p. 168). At this stage, problem recognition is contingent upon culture in the sense that some cultures take longer to acknowledge or express problems, whereas other cultures immediately address concerns, issues, or problems at hand. Kingdon's corresponding stage is agenda setting in which his concept of *agenda* alludes to the subject(s) being announced before a meeting begins. He defines agenda as "...coherent sets of proposals, each related to the others and forming the series of enactments its proponents would prefer" (1995, p. 3). He also suggests that agenda can mean the list of subjects or problems that need to be taken seriously at any given time. In this respect, the word agenda implies a sense of urgency.

The second step is to search for information once problems were identified. Adler posits that there are two forms of thinking when it comes to information gathering—(1) using logical order or (2) using intuition. Those people who use logical thinking gather information based on facts. On the contrary, people who use intuition or affective thinking gather ideas and possibilities based on relationship. Kingdon did not have a specific stage that is dedicated for information search, but his second step, called alternatives, does include this process.

The third step is to specify or construct the alternatives from which a choice is to be made. In this step, serious consideration is given to all potential alternatives. Adler suggests that once people have gathered sufficient and relevant information, they will begin to construct ideas or make proposals in order to address the problems identified. This process is shaped by the participants' cultural backgrounds since it raises questions such as whether the alternatives are composed of predominantly new ideas or ideas that are rooted in the past and whether it favors ideas that demand large or moderate (or no) amounts of change. Once ideas are presented, people respond by challenging or supporting the ideas, which may result in alternatives being modified or removed from consideration. Kingdon (1995) argued that at this stage, "...the process of specifying alternatives narrows the set of conceivable alternatives to the set that is seriously considered" (p. 4). During this crucial stage, experts brainstorm to generate as many solutions as possible, while the preceding agenda-setting stage is normally taken up by a leader.

The fourth step is concerned with making an authoritative choice among the specified alternatives. In this stage, Adler suggests making a decision from the range of presented and debated options. For Adler, several questions can be investigated here, such as who makes the decision, how fast decisions are made, at what level decisions are made, how much risk is involved, in what order people discuss alternatives, and when people select particular alternatives. As in all the steps, these questions also have cultural variations. This corresponds to Kingdon's (1995) third step in which he asserted that the most important thing is to understand how and why agenda items were selected for discussion in the first place, a question of "how they came to be issues" rather than "how issues are authoritatively decided by president, Congress, or other decision makers" (p. 2). This requires searching out for the underlying reasons why certain agenda items got picked over others; this is not an easy task since, as Kingdon (1995) puts it, "when a subject gets hot for a time, it is not always easy even in retrospect to discern why" (p. 2).

The final step in both Kingdon's and Adler's model is implementation, which provides closure to the actions that were taken in steps 1 through 4. This study did not analyze the implementation step since the focus of the study was process, not product. In the first phase of WSIS (Geneva), the final decisions were made by the government, so no decisions made among and within Civil Society members in the listserv were final or binding. Until the government made its decision, no implementation could take place; thus, this stage was not applicable in the context of Civil Society participation in the WSIS Geneva process.

In order to provide a general understanding of WSIS and the magnitude of the activities that took place in the period of 33 months, I will first describe the activities that took place in the Civil Society plenary listserv during the WSIS (see the "Active Months of Participation" section). Subsequently, in the said section, I will only focus on the WSIS Civil Society decision-making processes during WSIS Geneva and then compare the empirical model with the adapted models of Kingdon and Adler.

The WSIS listserv generated a total of 8,335 email messages from March 2003 to December 2005 (see Figure 7.3). This massive amount of email messages points out the significance of distributed collaborations among and within Civil Society participants in the WSIS process. On a broader perspective, participation was not constant during that period; there were months that generated heavy email traffic, whereas there

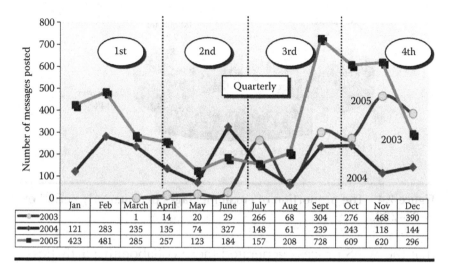

	Jan	Feb	March	April	May	June	July	Aug	Sept	Oct	Nov	Dec
2003			1	14	20	29	266	68	304	276	468	390
2004	121	283	235	135	74	327	148	61	239	243	118	144
2005	423	481	285	257	123	184	157	208	728	609	620	296

Figure 7.3   Email participation of Civil Society in WSIS Geneva and Tunis.

were months that generated less traffic. For example, during WSIS Geneva, November (n = 468) and December (n = 390) generated the heaviest traffic because the summit took place in December 2003, so the collaborative efforts were gearing up for the summit event. Similarly, in WSIS Tunis, the few months before and during the summit in 2005, September (n = 728), October (n = 609), and November (n = 620), showed a higher number of messages compared to any other preceding months. The face-to-face preparatory conferences and regional meetings also corresponded with and contributed to an increase in email discussions (see Figure 7.3).

On the overall situational analysis of email use (see Figure 7.3) from 2003 to 2005, the last four months of the year (n = 4,435) showed a heavy traffic of messages. For example, September (n = 1,271), October (n = 1,128), November (n = 1,206), and December (n = 830) all generated large numbers of email messages. These months accounted for 53% of the total messages. Some months were obviously less active such as from March to May (n = 1,144), which accounted for only 14% of the total messages. Looking at the quarterly trend for the period between 2003 and 2005 (see Figure 7.4), it is evident

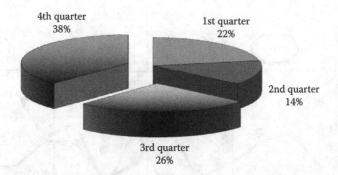

Figure 7.4 The proportion of email messages per quarterly period of 2003–2005.

that the WSIS process generated more collaborative activities during the third and fourth quarter of the year, respectively, 38% and 26%, which means that 64% of the collaborative efforts were inclined toward the last six months of the year. This time of the year also corresponded with the face-to-face meetings preceding PrepCom 3 and the summit events.

As Figure 7.5 shows, there was a regular increase in the number of email messages throughout WSIS Geneva and Tunis. In 2003, the archival messages totaled 1,836, which

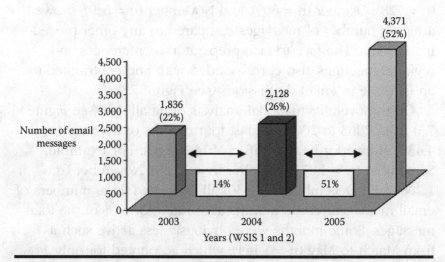

Figure 7.5 Civil Society email participation in WSIS process (2003–2005).

represented 22% of the total messages. In 2004, the total messages increased to 2,128, a minimal increase of only 14%, which represented 26% of total messages. In 2005, the number of messages was 4,371, an increase of 51%, which was almost twice the number of messages than the previous year. This 2005 total accounted for 52% of the bulk of the email traffic over the three-year period. With the increase in email messages from one year to another, it is evident that Civil Society used email as the primary tool not only for communication but also for collaboration, enabling them to effectively participate and contribute to the decision-making process in the WSIS.

Active Months of Participation

As shown in Figure 7.6b, the empirical findings of the study only focused on Civil Society participation in the virtual plenary listservs in WSIS Geneva. WSIS Geneva had a total of 1,836 messages with 223 Civil Society participants participating in the email listserv from April to December 2003. Figure 7.6a

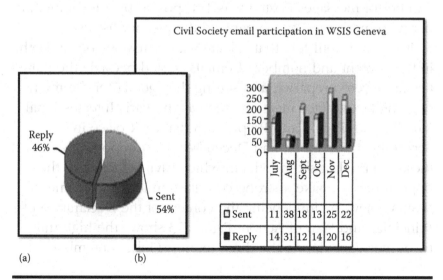

(a)　　　　(b)

Figure 7.6 (a) Proportion of sent and reply messages (July–December 2003). (b) Active months of participation.

shows that there were few email messages from April to June 2003—a total of 63 messages, representing only 4% of the total messages. These months were slow since those were the months when the email listserv was just set up by Civil Society plenary. Officially, the listserv was created in April 2003, although the preparatory meetings for both WSIS events took place much earlier via physical or face-to-face meetings (see Figure 7.3). The few emails were not substantial in content; in fact, most of the email was an auto-reply message in April and May. In June, there were a small number of discussions centered on the preparation for the meeting in Paris, the structure of Civil Society, and the issue of translation.

Therefore, the analysis was conducted on data from a six-month period (July to December 2003) because these were the most active months in terms of observable online communicative and collaborative behaviors. As seen in Figure 7.6b, Civil Society participants posted 1,760 email messages with 222* participants from July to December 2003. On average, eight messages were posted by each member over the six-month period or 1.33 messages each month. The maximum number of messages posted was 121, posted by a focal member who moderated and organized the plenary listserv.

It was not until July that substantial discussions began both in the content and number of emails posted because the participants were preparing and setting the agenda for the many ongoing face-to-face meetings such as the Paris Intersessional Meeting in mid-July and PrepCom 3 that took place in September, November, and December. Most importantly, these are the last six months in which Civil Society had the opportunity to make a strong contribution to the outcome of WSIS Geneva by influencing the content of the Declaration of Principles and Plan of Action. Figure 7.3 shows the high traffic of messages during the three months (July, September, and

---

* Only one participant did not continue to participate in the listserv from July onward.

November) surrounding the important events outside the email discussions as mentioned earlier in this section. The increment observed in those three months represented almost 50% of the total email messages, which indicated the importance of those three months.

Figure 7.6a shows an analysis of the CMC participation in terms of the messages sent and messages replied by Civil Society participants. The analysis shows that the messages posted outnumber the replied messages, 54% to 46%. However, there were not many differences between the two activities (n = 144), which accounted for only 8% of the total messages.

Distribution of Active Participants

Based on the average number of emails, the findings showed that 57 Civil Society participants were active participants in the WSIS Geneva process (see Table 7.1). As mentioned in the "Active Months of Participation" section, on average, each participant posted eight messages during the six-month period. Active participants, for this analysis, are defined as those that generated above the average number of emails (n = 8). Hence, for the six-month period, only 25% of the total membership (n = 222) were considered active participants out of the total number of participants in the plenary listserv. The active participants generated a total of 1,351 messages. Although the percentage of active participants was low, they generated 77% of the total volume of emails posted (n = 1,760). Each active

Table 7.1 Overall Patterns of Civil Society Participation: July–December 2003

Activities	Total
Total email messages sent by all participants	1,760 mails
Total number of participants during six months	222 participants
Average message sent per participant	7.93 = 8 mails

Table 7.2 Overview of Active Participation: July–December 2003

Activities	Total
Total number of active participants	57 participants
Total email messages sent by active participants	1,351 mails
Average message sent per active participant	24 mails
Average message sent per month by all active participants	225 mails

member sent out an average of 24 messages during the six-month period, and active participants generated an average of 224 mails per month (see Table 7.2).

As shown in Table 7.3, there were three key people who sent the highest number of emails—Kathryn Betty* (n = 121), Rolf Bauer (n = 77), and Rince Plum (n = 61). It was not surprising that Kathryn Betty was the most active participant because she was the listserv moderator, and the other two participants were also moderators for other listservs.

In a more detailed analysis, Figure 7.7 shows that the distribution of active participants fell into three groups. The first cluster of participants contained the three key people who were mentioned earlier in this section. These three made up only 5% of the total participants. Kathryn contributed 121 messages, an average of 20 messages each month, while Rolf contributed 77 messages, an average of 13 messages each month, and Rince contributed 61 messages, an average of 10 messages each month. The differences in number of messages sent were significant: between Kathryn and Rolf, a difference of 50 emails, while between Rolf and Rince, a difference of 15 emails.

The second cluster contained 18% of participants (n = 10), who posted from 28 to 57 messages; the difference in number

* Please note that in order to protect the confidentiality of the participating Civil Society, all the names used in this study are fictitious names. Although the data were taken from a public email archival, an initiative was taken to create pseudo-names for all of the participants.

Table 7.3   Distribution of Active Participation from Civil Society Participants: July–December 2003

Pseudo-Names	No. of Mails	No. of Participants
Kathryn Betty	121	1
Rolf Bauer	77	1
Rince Plum	61	1
Amanda Diego	54	1
Mariette Michel	53	1
Ruben Gerald	51	1
Blanche Baldemar	50	1
Jaquelin Floss	47	1
Benjamin Ines	42	1
Allan Patrick	41	1
Sandra Burkasa	39	1
Vince Markow	37	1
Fedrick Marlin	30	1
Adrian Alfonso	27	1
Percy Fernand	26	1
Edul Zaki	25	1
Gerard Grosvenor	24	1
Samuel Charles, Renee Blusky	23	2
James Grutan	21	1
Wutz Kaiser	22	1
Alim Baruki, Njemile Negas, Steven Osborne, Venda Busara	20	4
Rick Weissmen	19	1

(Continued)

Table 7.3 (Continued)   Distribution of Active Participation from Civil Society Participants: July–December 2003

Pseudo-Names	No. of Mails	No. of Participants
Emilio Marco, Verner Vinson	17	2
Kim Soon	16	1
Anita Johnson, Timothy Rhodes, Yihong Chang	14	3
Jihong Mun, Patrick Adler, Morty Bijou, Albert Jonathan, Ellen Carlson, David Betrand	13	6
Vesa Parnella, Raymond Jacob, Jimmy Punnel, Denise Merraga	12	4
Melanie Milagros	11	1
Butler Parnell, Charlie Nahum, Daniella Freud, Dawana Franks, Hokaido Kanagam, Tina Numen, Rudelle Franzisca	10	7
Nadim Salman, Crsytal Shaw, Rolan Kiefer	9	3
Emma Joshua, Isuzuki Akito, Stanford James, Tamara Antonia	8	4
Total	**1,351**	**57**

of emails sent by each of them was not significant, a difference of only one or two emails. The last cluster showed the largest proportion of the participants, 77%.

Participants in this cluster sent 27 or fewer messages, an average of only 4.5 messages each month.

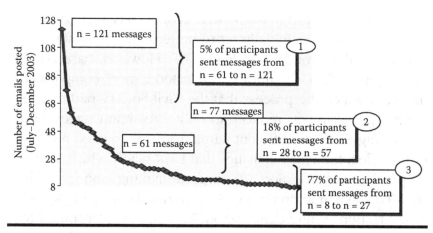

Figure 7.7 Distribution of active Civil Society members in virtual plenary listserv.

Distribution of Less Active Participants

There were 165 participants that were considered as less active participants. They sent less than the average number of emails, a range from one to seven emails. The total number of emails contributed by them (n = 409) accounted for only 23% of the total emails posted in the listserv. In spite of the low number of emails sent, 80 of them did actually contribute to the decision-making process ranging from 1 to 5 messages and a total of 187 messages. Again, this number is still lower than the representation of the total participants who participated in the virtual plenary listserv during WSIS Geneva.

During the WSIS, Civil Society participants made numerous and wide-ranging decisions either individually or collectively during their face-to-face meetings. This study's findings suggest that a similar process took place in the globally distributed environment that is particularly focused on the WSIS Geneva. The following empirical model of decision-making process is a revised version of the initial framework (see Figure 7.1). As illustrated in Figure 7.8, the decision-making model was adapted from Adler (1997) and Kingdon (1995). The model clearly depicts the activities that took place over the six-month period in the virtual Civil Society plenary list-serv. The study was initially set to understand a four-stage decision-making model (see Figure 7.1). However, based on the empirical data, the findings indicated a more complicated model in which the process that the Civil Society participants were engaged in was reduced to only three main stages. Each of the stages used a different name from the adapted models to reflect the exact activities that took place, which are (1) problem identification, (2) proposal making, and (3) solution. This dynamic process was supported by a fourth stage called responses and deliberation. This stage underpinned the other three activities because every response received was fed into the decision-making process until a viable solution was achieved. Although Adler and Kingdon had a sequential model, I found that Civil Society participants were engaged in a more dynamic and iterative process in which the responses and deliberation occurred continuously.

In the first stage, one or more participants would state a problem, followed by other participants responding to the problem by proposing solutions. Most of the time, participants

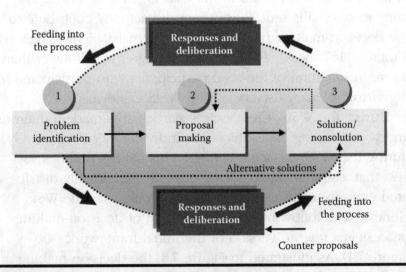

Figure 7.8 Empirical model of globally distributed Civil Society decision-making processes during WSIS Geneva.

came up with many ideas and suggestions on how to solve the problems faced or how to improve a draft document. At other times, participants simply acknowledged problems without offering any ideas or solutions—for example, "I do experience the same problem" or "I agree with your sentiment." Under rare circumstances, a problem was immediately resolved because a leader took independent or unilateral actions without going through the proposal stage.

For the second stage, once proposals were made by the participants, the proposals received reactions or feedback from other participants; sometimes, this generated more ideas and alternative solutions. If people were supportive of the proposed language in the draft document, then they would endorse the draft document. But, if some participants did not agree with the suggested proposals, then counterproposals would be presented in a search for more viable solutions. This stage was often a long process as participants took the time to really look at the document and then provide thoughtful suggestions on how to improve it. Sometimes, however, the process was shortened because the document needed to be finalized within time constraints. In this iterative process, the multitude of responses received eventually led to the best solution that participants could offer.

For the third stage, solution took one of two forms. When participants faced a problem, the solution took the form of actions to remedy the situations or issues faced. For example, participants requested and received answers that clarified their concerns, or action was taken by the authoritative people (like the bureau or secretariat) to provide facilities needed. Sometimes, alternative solutions were proposed when participants were not satisfied with the offered solution. If there is an agenda to be met, like providing comments to a draft document or selecting or nominating speakers, then a different set of solutions is achieved. For such agenda-driven issues, the solution came in the form of endorsements. The more and the faster endorsements were received, the easier for the

Civil Society to reach consensus. For example, in the case of a speaker's selection, participants went through many cycles of nomination and counternomination; the solution was achieved when the name of the speaker was finalized. In some cases, despite the participants' best efforts, proposals were made, and suggestions were given, but no solution was achieved; the decision-making process failed.

The decision-making process that Civil Society participants engage in via globally distributed collaboration occurs at the individual level—between and among participating Civil Society participants. Thus, the first assumption was to examine the decision-making process based not on the cognitive level but rather on the interaction level. Another important assumption was that the process is mediated by the use of CMC (in this case, by email). The last assumption was that decision making is based on consensus and not unanimity. Consensus means that only the participants engaged or involved in the process need to agree to the propositions, whereas unanimity means all the Civil Society participants must agree regardless whether or not they are involved in the process. This was hard to achieve via the email participation of Civil Society in the WSIS. For a consensus, the involved participants must come forward and endorse the proposals being made.

In essence, I would like to make the distinction between those two concepts clearly because, in the context of Civil Society participation on the WSIS email lists, people voluntarily work on a draft of proposal documents and propositions, which may lead to various decision points during the interim face-to-face meetings leading up to the WSIS event. After proposals were made, participants were free to react to the propositions. Solutions and decisions were made when consensus was reached. (Only the people who had read and participated in the process needed to endorse or agree to it.) Decisions were not based on unanimity wherein all the participants registered on the email list would have been required to endorse the proposals, nor did the process include all the

Civil Society organizations in the WSIS. The email list was used to get as much agreement as possible so that actions can be taken or draft documents can be shaped, but was not presumed or required to result in unanimity.

References

Adler, N.J. 1997. *International Dimensions of Organizational Behavior*, 3rd ed. Cincinnati, OH: South-Western.

Kingdon, J.W. 1995. *Agendas, Alternatives, and Public Policies*. New York: Addison-Wesley Longman.

Saaty, T.L. 2012. *Decision Making for Leaders: The Analytic Hierarchy Process for Decisions in a Complex World*. Pittsburgh, PA: RWS Publication.

Chapter 8

Problem Identification

Civil Society's Contributions in the Decision-Making Processes

In this section, the following analysis looks at the proportion of messages in each of the three distinct stages of the decision-making processes (see Figure 8.1) and Civil Society global virtual team (GVT) members' contributions in the process. In the "Problem Identification Process" section, I will describe the way Civil Society engaged in the problem identification processes and how high-context members differ from low-context members in the manner that they identify and understand problems, as well as the techniques that they apply when dealing with problems that were encountered during their discussions.

Problem identification (n = 479) accounted for 44%, proposal making (n = 497) accounted for 45%, and solution (n = 119) accounted for only 11% of all total decision-making activities. Together, problem identification and proposal-making activities made up 89% of the activities. This high proportion strongly suggests that Civil Society participants were committed in identifying issues that arose specifically within their collaboration, as well as sharing their proposals, ideas, and

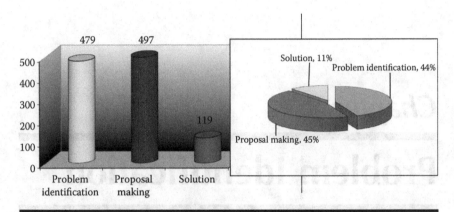

Figure 8.1   Distribution and proportion of the decision-making activities in WSIS Geneva.

suggestions arising from their expertise in order to influence the language of the two key documents (Declaration of Principles and Plan of Action), which were the outcome of WSIS Geneva.

In addition, the findings showed a total of 1,095 messages related to decision-making activities, or 62% of the total messages (N = 1,760) in the six-month period. Out of the 57 participants identified as active Civil Society participants (see Table 8.3), almost all of them (96%, n = 55) contributed to the decision-making activities. Specifically, contributions made by active participants accounted for 83% (n = 908) of the decision-making messages, while many fewer contributions were made by less active participants, representing a mere 17% (n = 187) of the messages.

Further analysis of decision-making messages indicated that not all the messages posted by the active participants were related to the decision-making process. As illustrated in Table 8.1, active participants contributed a total of 1,351 messages to the listserv. About 67% of their messages were related to decision, while only a small portion (33%) was contributed to the nonrelated decision-making activities. The following result showed the breakdown of two categories of participants that contributed to two categories of activities—(1) decision- and

Table 8.1 Distribution of Messages for Decision and Non-Decision-Making Activities between Active and Less Active Participants

Participants/Activities	Active Participants	Less Active Participants	Total
Decision-making	908 mails	187 mails	1,095 mails
Non-decision-making	443 mails	222 mails	665 mails
Total	1,351 mails	409 mails	1,760 mails

(2) non-decision-related activities based on the number of emails contributed. The result showed that, in general, active participants contributed far many more than less active participants. By looking at the total number of emails each group contributed, it is also apparent that active participants generated far more decision-making and non-decision-making messages than the less active participants, a difference of almost 70%.

The subsequent findings further detailed the degree of effectiveness of active participants based on several analyses. The analysis was made based on 55 active participants (see Table 8.2). Two of the active participants did not contribute to the decision-making process. About 58% of the active participants (n = 35) participated in all three stages of the decision-making process. And two participants, Wutz Kaiser and James Grutan, contributed 100% of their messages to the three stages of the decision-making process. In terms of the ranking based on the number of messages devoted to decision making, Kathryn Betty was still ranked as the highest contributor to the process, and she participated in all the activities, especially in the solution stage.

Not all participants (n = 20) contributed their efforts in all three stages. Participants who engaged in only two stages are shown in Table 8.3. Note that even though these participants did not engage in all three phases of the decision-making process, particularly the *solution* stage, the majority of them contributed actively to the first two stages. In fact, for three of

Table 8.2 Ranking and Distribution of Active Participants for All Decision-Making Stages

| | Total Mails | Stages of Decision Making | | | % of Messages Related to Decision Making |
		Problem	Proposal	Solution	
Kathryn Betty	81	35	24	22	67%
Mariette Michel	49	28	18	3	92%
Rolf Bauer	41	19	20	2	53%
Rince Plum	39	18	13	8	64%
Blanche Baldemar	39	20	16	3	78%
Vince Markow	34	17	13	4	92%
Sandra Burkasa	34	18	25	3	87%
Jaquelin Floss	34	14	17	3	72%
Allan Patrick	33	13	18	2	80%
Amanda Diego	31	13	17	1	57%
Fedrick Marlin	26	10	14	2	87%
Wutz Kaiser	22	9	11	2	100%
Percy Fernand	21	8	11	2	81%

(Continued)

Table 8.2 (Continued) Ranking and Distribution of Active Participants for All Decision-Making Stages

| | Total Mails | Stages of Decision Making | | | % of Messages Related to Decision Making |
		Problem	Proposal	Solution	
James Grutan	21	9	9	3	100%
Adrian Alfonso	21	6	11	4	78%
Benjamin Ines	20	8	8	4	48%
Ruben Gerald	19	5	12	2	37%
Alim Baruki	18	11	6	1	90%
Renee Blusky	16	1	8	7	70%
Samuel Charles	14	7	5	2	61%
Morty Bijou	12	4	7	1	92%
Butler Parnell	9	6	2	1	90%
Albert Jonathan	9	3	5	1	69%
Vesa Parnella	8	4	2	2	67%
David Betrand	8	4	3	1	62%
Stanford Barnes	7	2	3	2	88%

(Continued)

Table 8.2 (Continued) Ranking and Distribution of Active Participants for All Decision-Making Stages

| | Total Mails | Stages of Decision Making | | | % of Messages Related to Decision Making |
		Problem	Proposal	Solution	
Kim Soon	7	3	2	2	44%
Isuzuki Akito	7	2	4	1	88%
Hokaido Kanagama	7	4	2	1	70%
Daniella Freud	7	2	3	2	70%
Patrick Adler	6	2	3	1	46%
Edul Zaki	6	1	4	1	24%
Emma Joshua	5	1	3	1	63%
Crystal Shaw	4	1	2	1	44%
Charlie Nahum	3	1	1	1	30%

Table 8.3 Ranking and Distribution of Participants Who Participated in Two Decision-Making Stages

	Total Mails	Stages of Decision Making			% of Messages Related to Decision Making
		Problem	Proposal	Solution	
Steven Osborne	20	8	12		100%
Gerard Grosvenor	20	10	10		83%
Rick Weissmen	16	5	11		84%
Yihong Chang	14	9	5		100%
Venda Busara	13	7	6		65%
Ellen Carlson	12	4	8		92%
Anita Johnson	11	4	7		79%
Raymond Jacob	10	4	6		83%
Rolan Kiefer	9	5	4		100%
Nadim Salman	8	3	5		89%
Njemile Negash	7	5	2		35%
Tina Numen	6	5	1		60%

(Continued)

Table 8.3 (Continued)   Ranking and Distribution of Participants Who Participated in Two Decision-Making Stages

	Total Mails	Stages of Decision Making			% of Messages Related to Decision Making
		Problem	Proposal	Solution	
Verner Vinson	5	1	4		29%
Timothy Rhodes	5	4		1	36%
Emilio Marco	5	3		2	29%
Denise Merraga	5	4		9	75%
Rudelle Franziska	3	1	2		30%
Melanie Milagros	2		2		18%
Jimmy Punnel	2		2		17%
Tamara Antonia	1		1		13%

the participants—(1) Steven, (2) Yihong, and (3) Rolan—100% of their messages concerned some phase of decision making, either actively addressing problems or making proposals, as well as responding to them.

Problem Identification Process

According to Adler (1997), the process of decision making begins with problem recognition, which I refer to as *problem identification*. The findings showed that there were two types of situations that took place during this early stage of decision making: (1) Civil Society participants discussed their problems and concerns, and (2) Civil Society participants discussed an agenda that was clearly identified— for example, based on a list of problems or topics to be addressed. After a problem was brought up by a member, other participants began to respond to it by either providing their ideas and opinions or making suggestions. Some responses were simply feedback or comments about the problem identified, but some were more concrete suggestions on how to solve the problems. It is important to note that at this stage, Civil Society participants only responded to the problems that were identified by others. If a problem was not clearly raised or mentioned in the email, then the issue could not be discussed. Thus, this initial stage is critical because unless and until people identify the problems, a solution could not be achieved. The findings also showed that agenda-driven discussions seemed to make the decision-making process within and among the Civil Society participants go in a more directed manner and got discussed more often.

As Figure 8.2 shows, problem identification instances were highest in November (n = 143) and December (n = 103). This pattern is consistent with the overall pattern of Civil Society participation in WSIS Geneva. Overall, the central topic of

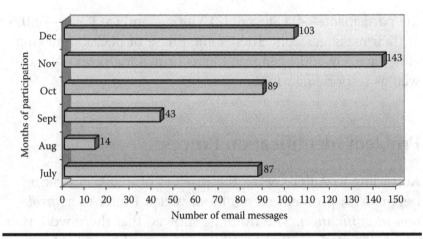

Figure 8.2 Problem identification activities in WSIS Geneva.

discussion throughout the six months was the language of the two primary documents—Declaration of Principles and Plan of Action. However, there was also a distinct agenda in some of the months. For example, in July (n = 87), participants were concerned about the setup of the infrastructure such as the availability of computers, Internet, and wireless connections; working space and room; and the structure and mechanism of the Civil Society. In November, participants were more concerned about the nomination of the speakers, as well as the time slot, and, in December, they focused on finalizing the language of the document, as well as selecting their speaker, in order to be fully prepared for the summit that took place in mid-December 2003.

The problems that Civil Society participants identified in WSIS Geneva include the following:

■ *Infrastructure*—technology issues on connectivity, wireless, and logistics such as meeting room and working space
■ *Language*—the problem of using English in email, translations, and the use of other non-English language such as using Spanish, French, or any other United Nations (UN) languages
■ *Structure*—the mechanism, organization, and coordination for civil society

- *Resources*—giving out badges or limited passes for entrance to PrepComs' meetings and the WSIS
- *Coordination*—problems in coordinating the efforts within civil society in terms of sending the comments of the document, and deadlines to submit comments
- *Procedures*—formatting issues on sending drafts, where and how to send documents

Table 8.4 provides more detailed examples of problem identification statements based on the WSIS emails.

Additionally, Civil Society participants were engaged in the agenda-driven discussions in respect of (1) the language of the two drafted documents and (2) the nomination of speakers— a participant who is chosen by consensus to represent Civil Society participants in the summit. The main goal was to influence these two documents. The findings indicated that a member in a leadership role often took up the task of *agenda setting*, and this role is based on his or her own initiative. The leader would set a certain agenda and request attention and/or action from the Civil Society participants. For example, Benjamin clearly set an agenda by asking for comments for a draft document as follows:

> All*,
> Attached is the latest draft of the Civil Society priorities document for Paris. Please send comments by Friday to ct@wsis-cs.org.
>   We must produce the final document by the weekend.
>
> BI

---

* Please note that any typographical error or grammatical structures existed in the messages will not be corrected because the excerpts were taken directly from the data set. However, the only exception is that when messages include organizational names or any other important events in which all of that specific information will be removed or left blank in the messages as quoted in this study.

Table 8.4   Examples of Problem Identification Statements

Types of Problems	Quotations from Email Messages
a. Infrastructure	• "Many thanks for this. Will there be computers in the drafting room? And will there be any Internet access other than the Internet cafe (which presumably will be much in demand)?" • "Can Civil Society representatives who are also accredited under a govt. delegation enter the room? If so, might they be able to relay us the news using Wireless?"
b. Language	• "Saras and Anita echo your concerns and also raise the issue of Portuguese-speaking participants?" • "The Content & Themes group needs help to produce translations prior to the meeting. CT has one member working on the French version, but could use assistance. We have not yet identified people for other languages."
c. Structure and Mechanism of CS	• "I am sorry but I do not see why we need to discuss the structure of CS again, coming back to issues that have previously already been clarified. I do fully agree with you that transparency is very important, but I believe the current system, where the CS Contents and Themes Group, as well as the CS Bureau report back to the CS Plenary works just fine." • "Certainly, issues such as Jeffrey Gerber's comments on the Plenary, if he is to chair the Bureau, need clarification and agreement—they cannot be ignored. And this is a non-contentious way of doing that which all sides the integrity of their views."

(Continued)

Table 8.4 (Continued)   Examples of Problem Identification Statements

Types of Problems	Quotations from Email Messages
d. Resources	• "I've followed the exchanges regarding the issue of passes for the summit. They express the latest scandal regarding the process." • "What are these photo badges? Does that mean that they will take a photo during registration or is that a new kind of badge that we should ask for? Also, should all the accredited organization contact ict4d? What for, another kind of badge?"
e. Coordination	• "We discussed the need to work immediately on coordination and logistics plan for PrepCom III. Lisa Larry has asked that we submit at least a rough outline of our logistical needs this week. Rolf Bauer has drafted a document outlining these needs, based on discussions at the end of PrepCom II and as a result of our experiences during the Intersessional." • "This is good strategic document that I think gets us closer to the kind of coordinated functioning that Civil Society should aim towards. However, in terms of what is possible to get together between now and September, I think your overall scheme is ambitious. Let me suggest something perhaps more achievable."

(Continued)

Table 8.4 (Continued)   Examples of Problem Identification Statements

Types of Problems	Quotations from Email Messages
f. Procedures	• "I think there should be joint discussions on this and other questions of common concern, so I am circulating to these lists (there are no contentious personal views, I hope). It concerns guidelines for the allocation of speaker slots at the PrepComs etc." • "We have put the CS priorities document online at http://www.worldsummit2003.de /download_en/WSIS-CS-CT-Paris-071203.rtf. We also have produced an overview with all practical infos on the Paris meeting, including a timetable with the (so far) announced CS activities. I will be in Paris from tomorrow evening and report for our web site on a daily basis. Check http://www.worldsummit 2003.org for more updates and news in the next days."

The data also showed that in certain situations, people responded to the agenda at different times. Some agenda generated many responses, whereas others did not even get a response; this seemed to depend on the nature of the agenda and whether it caught the participants' attention. For the three months that generated the highest number of instances, the participants responded more vigorously because there was a deadline in the agenda (for example, language for the drafted documents or problems regarding the infrastructure).

Adler (1997) suggests that once people recognize a problem, the next stage is *information search*, a question of how people find and gather information to solve the problem. In WSIS Geneva, this stage was obvious during the iterative response to and deliberation on the problem or agenda, so, in this study, the information search stage is actually embedded in the response and deliberation stage. Therefore, I did not explicitly differentiate the information search stage in the empirical model.

Problem Identification Behaviors

The key question here is to understand the manner in which people express the concerns, issues, or problems that they faced in the WSIS Geneva. High-context participants presented their problems without using the word *problem* explicitly in their email. Neither did they use words like *concerns* or *issues*. Instead, they used ambiguous phrases like "I am afraid that…" or "perhaps it would be…" Another approach was either using polite gestures in the message like "thank you for the great work…" or apologizing, such as "I am sorry for not describing the whole scene…" Only then would they be comfortable in presenting the problems.

Even then, they still stated the essence of their concerns indirectly. For example, high-context participants usually provided lengthy messages about a problem. Sometimes, the problems or concerns were so deeply buried in the anecdotal stories that the substance of the problem was lost. Because the problem was blurred and not concisely stated, it was not taken seriously by the participants. For example, in Yihong Chang's email, although his initial tone was direct, the words "I attach the outcome…" camouflage his real intention, which was to voice his concerns. Before expressing that concern, he offered an apology ("I am sorry") and then proceeded with his concerns followed by a series of questions before he asserted his views. The following is a short excerpt of Yihong's email from a longer version:

> Here, I attach the outcome of the ad-hoc working group of Internet Governance.
>
> Bracket part has not yet reached to an agreement.

I was told that the key conflicting part was number 4. (a) was proposed by the U.S. (b) was proposed by Brazil and China. And some countries made comments to delete the phrase of "under the UN framework," so the remaining phrase is (c). Canada proposed (e) and EU and some other countries amended that proposal by deleting the phrase of "mutually agreed."

I am sorry. This explanation was not given by official briefing.

Still, I have not heard any notification from that working group.

I should have tried to collect information what has been done behind the curtain. In this case, Internet or some ICTs are not helpful at all.

Could you solve this puzzle? What could be final consensus? In my view, the final consensus, if it could be, would be reached to coming December Summit. Quite frankly, I could not guess the possible compromise of these conflicting views. Anyhow, I am thinking the riddle of power balance and reason/understanding. My internal question is if we are going towards information and communication society or is it really progress of human beings?

Yihong Chang

In essence, high-context participants were not comfortable expressing their concerns forthrightly, which made their emails longer than those of low-context participants. The participants had to read such email closely in order to understand the main concerns. Sometimes, a message contained many concerns, and, as a consequence, the messages failed to address the main, urgent problems that required actions or solutions.

This is a different strategy from that used by low-context participants, who are more likely to jump into the matter immediately with a short question. Low-context people usually expressed their concerns *straight to the point* and used succinct wording. They sent messages with questions that pertained only to the concerns that they had or the problems that they encountered. Hence, low-context participants generally sent short messages like "Is there any wireless connection?" or "Will it be possible to connect our computers there?" Sometimes, the message included an explicit request regarding issues that concerned the plenary listserv participants such as the following from Denise Merraga:

> I think that this issue is raging on and on. I know that people need to have the opportunity to choose and express opinions. I think that there also comes a time when the additions have to stop and we have to look at the list we have and choose.
> Please let's get to that point soon.
>
> Denise

The brevity, relevance, and preciseness of such a communication style did capture the attention of other participants, as evidenced by the fact that the message received responses and solutions. For example, in regard to the wireless problem, Kathryn and Renee immediately took actions and solved the problem. Another example is that of Emilio, "Hello there, I cannot access the link you had provided…" Kathryn jumped straight away into the discussion and offered help on what to do. This is a classic example of a low-context person's task-oriented way to solve the problem.

There were variations in the manner in which low-context people responded to a problem that arose or a concern that was expressed by the participants. For example, one member raised her concerns about the process and deadlines for registration. Benjamin responded,

> I think the deadline was only for the fellowships.
> I do not think that the travel information is necessary

to complete the registration. I am a focal point and
have successfully registered someone without that
information. It may also be possible to go back and
update the information. I am not sure though.

And Michael answered,

My reading of the WSIS website instructions is that
while the organizations registering persons must
have met the now-past deadline for accreditation,
accredited organizations can even register persons
at the desk on opening day. There are instructions
there for both pre-registration and on-site registration.

Although the low-context people were precise in the manner that they posted problems or expressed their concerns,
some of the responses were so terse as to seem hostile and
blunt. For example, Samuel further responded in a harsh
manner to Michael and Benjamin with an opening statement,
such as

Not my understanding. December 3rd is the final
date for accredited organizations to add people to
their list of delegates.

Another succinct proposal arose when Civil Society participants discussed the issue of creating the North American/
European caucus. Some participants voiced their disagreement,
and some seemed to be in favor of it. However, when Ruben's
message (as follows) was sent, it almost sounded like a solution, although it was a proposal made in response to the issue.
His message was crystal clear and sharp so that it is much
easier to notice the priority and urgency of the message. The
tone of the message sounded more like a command, yet there
is also a hint of persuasion when he used the words "I would
suggest…" He also used a semicolon after addressing Amanda,

like "Amanda" is the topic or subject matter rather than referring to Amanda as a person:

Amanda:

there already is a north-america/european cacus
group and mailing list for it. though it was late in
forming, it was involved in many activities at pc3.
    I would suggest joining that group.

Ruben

Not only were low-context participants precise in their email,
but they also did not waste a lot of time communicating what
they intended to get across to others. Their responses to problems can be simply providing people with the URL link when
they requested information or quoted a specific text from other
messages in order to reiterate a point or to clarify an issue that
was brought up. For example, many of James Grutan's responses
to problems were as terse as this sentence, "The Secretariat just
sent the tentative agenda. See below," followed by the messages
that he pasted into the text. Even though his email may be long,
actually, the rest of the message was a pasted one.

Most of the high- and low-context people demonstrated
consistent behavior throughout the six months. But some
of them switched. Fredrick typically portrayed high-context
behaviors, with an indirect manner of presenting his ideas and
expressing his opinions. But, occasionally, his style reversed
when he became more frustrated with the process. For, example, the following messages showed a more assertive style
when he responded to Jenny's and Mariette's proposal:

Dear Jenny & Mariette,
about what ? about what kind of message ? if the CS
speaker just speaks about generalities that are our
least common divisor, officials in the UN assembly

would certainly welcome it and felt relieved. Is this
what the CS really wants ?

This is going to disappoint many persons in the
whole world and specifically in emergent countries.

It is not required that the speaker be part of the
"system," be a former minister or some VIP, what is
important is the content of the message and from
that it should be determined what is the best speaker
to deliver it and NOT the reverse way around.

and doesn't put them off. for sure; some people
will be upset, so what ? it simply means that something important is dealt with.

I am not sure RS is the best choice for this task.

You are perfectly right, but it is the proposed task
which is not right in my views.

I personally suggest that this ridiculously small
amount of time: five minutes (the only ones that
would get world media coverage) must be put into
some good practical use, it may be by RS with software patents, it may be by Mariette calling for the
liberation of some imprisoned web masters, it may
be another issue, but I suggest that we should agree
to propose Opening speaker nominations based on
the requirement of a practical impact.

Best regards
Fedrick

The impact of culture on *problem identification* activities
can be summarized as follows:

■ If the problems were simple, easily fixed, and require
less demanding actions, the low-context messages with
short questions or concise statements generated more

responses from other participants than the ambiguous or indirect problem statement that is given by high-context messages.

■ If the problems were complicated and needed more ideas and/or consensus, high-context messages can be equally valuable and useful as low-context detailed messages because both types of behaviors would present persuasive and strong logical arguments.

Reference

Adler, N.J. 1997. *International Dimensions of Organizational Behavior*, 3rd ed. Cincinnati, OH: South-Western.

Chapter 9

Proposal Making

Introduction

The second stage is called proposal making in which participants contributed to a wide range of ideas and made a large number of inputs. In this stage, participants first presented their proposals, followed by the dynamic behaviors of proposing, receiving responses, criticizing, and deliberating, all of which exemplify what Adler (1997) and Kingdon (1995) referred to as *constructing or specifying alternatives*. This stage is crucial because the numerous responses ease the process of shaping constructive proposals in an attempt to find a solution. At any point in time, many people presented several options or alternatives. Then, participants discussed and deliberated on the ideas and suggestions at length. Similar to the problem identification stage, there were also times where ideas or proposals received no response or minimal response, whereas others received a very contentious response or highly supportive comments. Again, the responses depended largely on the types of proposals or ideas that were generated, whether it was acceptable or nonacceptable, or viable or nonviable, to follow through by the participants.

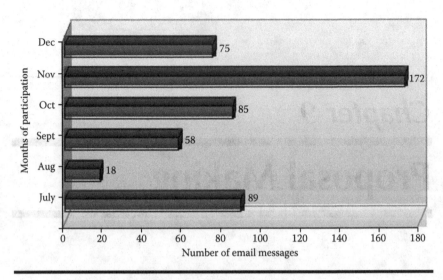

Figure 9.1 Proposal-making activities in WSIS Geneva.

The findings (see Figure 9.1) show that proposal-making activities were concentrated in July (n = 89), October (n = 85), and November (n = 172). The overall trend was similar to problem identification activities, but, this time, in December, the activity showed a decrease of more than 50% from the previous month.

The proposal-making activities arose from the problems discussed or agenda set in the plenary listserv. When the participants began to respond to the problems or agenda, they often presented ideas in the form of a proposal. The following are the examples of the many proposals that were made, as well as the responses that were received, in light of the two crucial agendas:

1. *Language to be included in the document*
   Proposal made:
   Dear All,
   We (—) propose to include at the end of the section: "Literacy, Education, and Research" next statement:
   [—should become "backbones" for nation-wide promotion and distribution of science and education

information covering all categories of inhabitants. Governments under must support them continuous programs of creating and maintaining research and education resources and services.]

Best regards,

Dr. Veache Siren

Response received:

Dear Dr Siren,

I'd just suggest that these networks also commit themselves in the inclusion and support of DCs Education networks (as far as there are or will be in a foreseeble future) and Institutions such as Universities, highschools and specially technical (Engineer) schools.

Why not stress particularly those institutions petraining to the ICT sector? This would be a positive act of solidarity between the North and the South (between "haves" and "have nots").

Regards,

Jaquelin Floss

2. *Nomination of speaker and time slot at the summit event*

Overall, the responses to the proposals made by Civil Society participants were encouraging. The responses were given in a continuum—from a positive scale up to a negative scale. On the extreme side of the positive scale, people were very supportive of the proposal made, and they fully backed up the suggestions and ideas that were given. For example, the following quotation from Adam indicated a positive response for a nominated speaker:

I strongly support the idea that the name of Mrs. Farah would be suggested to Secretary General Kofi Annan as well as to the president of the PrepComs and ITU for addressing the General Assembly of the WSIS on behalf of the CS.

Or a response from Sandy

Thank you for your comments regarding my prior message! I think Adrian is addressing one important procedural issue that we should take the decision making power to nominate for speaking slots. First, that should be sorted out. And basically fully agree with Alim that the nomination of Mrs. Farah for a key speaker could have very strong message itself. And IF we decide to use the speaking slots for our strategy, I fully support that idea.

Proposal-Making Behaviors

High-context participants began their proposals with a formal tone through the initial greetings and salutation, followed by a remark, which puts the statement in a context. For example, in responding to a drafted document, Rick Weissmen regretfully voiced his late response, only then suggesting a few things to be changed. It took 17 words before he stated, "I suggest…" He also justified the need for the changes in his closing statement.

May be I just too late.
About the non-paper of the president of the PrepCom
I suggest the following re-structuring, the articles numbers
I refer to are the one of this text:

1. Article 2 (Our challenge…) should be in part B and moved between 15 and 16, so become the first of Part B.
2. Point 8 (Cultural [identity] and diversity,….) and the articles 49, 50 and 51 have their place, eventually after being rewritten, in Part A between the actual articles 5 and 6.

    3. Point 10 (Ethical dimension.....) should also be moved to, eventually after being rewritten, to point A. (Our Vision...) between articles 6 and 7.
    4. Article 3 is a standard expression not really related to WSIS.

    I realize by looking into more detail of the text, that some additional redactional work remains to be done!
Cordially, Rick Weissmen

Rick sent another email right after that, and his style was still consistent. He maintained his subtle way of making suggestions and giving justification. In fact, in this email, he sounded more apologetic for the changes that he made and hoped that they would be considered.

    Dear all,
    In a previous mail I suggested some re-arrangements of the articles.
    In the attachment I did some re-shuffling, the changes are in red.
    However, I realize now that this is not enough. One should first work on a 'content' structure and then write texts around it.
    But it is perhaps too late, and the effort is considerable.
    Cordially,
    Rick Weissmen

Aside from the usual pattern of expressing gratitude early in the message, high-context participants also used an individual voice. But the individuality was not as strongly felt because it was made in reference to others. In that sense, it sounded more like a collective voice; for example, "But for the part Allan pointed out, I share the same concern" or "I share

Vince's opinion too." They also often used the pronouns *I* and *we* jointly in the same sentence (such as in the third paragraph as follows). Although Isuzuki seemed to establish a position by using the pronoun I, his statement was not assertive since he cushioned his views with words of uncertainty such as "I am afraid," "I guess," and "I hope..." The message from Isuzuki illustrates typical high-context behavior with lengthy explanations [emphasis added]:

Benjamin and all, I appreciate your hard work and good result.

But for the part Allan pointed out, I share the same concern.

I have been involved with ICANN since the very beginning, and mostly around "At Large" issues, and am still engaged as the interim member of the AtLarge Advisory Committee.

I agree that the current ICANN framework is far from the best solution and especially the civil society/individual user participation has been not fully accepted as **we** wanted to be.

Yet the current draft for Declaration and Action Plans prepared by WISI secretariat are quite dangerous in that it may lead stronger government intervention, or control under the "intergovernmental" body if adopted.

So the current language of the civil society document may further invite this government involvement in the way, under the name of "public interest" and all stakeholders, that further marginalize the civil society participation, **I am afraid**.

That is the point Allan is trying to explain, **I guess**. And I share Vince's opinion, too.

I hope you could consider this and will delete that para.

ICANN is certainly not perfect at all, but the government camps trying to change the current framework is much much worse.

Please remember that many innovations and freedom enjoyed around Internet have so far been made possible thanks to no government regulation/intervention.

IETF, ICANN, W3C et all are all part of this new ways of managing the Net.

Even though they did not have "enough" civil society participation, the Internet Community did much better job than government/industry-led standardizing body such as ITU.

Isuzuki

In Violet's message (as follows), she slowly introduced the subject matter before she expressed her disagreement. Again, it took almost 44 words before she apologetically expressed her ideas and views. The tone of the message became more intense in the third paragraph, as shown by her using capital letters (underlining added) to make sure that people understand her point. Toward the end of her message, she reiterated the point but with reference to Wutz's idea. This strategy softens her assertiveness because her individual voice was made in reference to someone else's.

Dear Steven,

CS has spent a great amount of energy discussing and rediscussing its structure. In Paris, CS managed to get a substantial amount of work done, and this at all three levels: the CS Plenary, the CS Contents and Themes Group and the CS Bureau.

I am sorry but I do not see why we need to discuss the structure of CS again, coming back to issues that have previously already been clarified. I do

fully agree with you that transparency is very impor-
tant, but I believe the current system, where the
CS Contents and Themes Group, as well as the CS
Bureau report back to the CS Plenary works just fine.
 This is why I do NOT see the need for a new task
force.
 **As pointed out by Wutz, the structure is as
follows:**

1. There is a "Civil Society Plenary" (CS-P), open to
   everybody, which is, as the name says, the main
   body of civil society, also for general decisions
   making.
2. There is a "Civil Society Content and Themes
   Group" (CS-CTG), which coordinates the work
   of the numerous caucuses and content groups.
   The CS-CTG is the main body for decisions on
   content related issues (by respecting, that the
   expertise and competence is in the caucuses and
   content working groups).
3. There is a "Civil Society Bureau" (CS-B), which
   functions as an interlinkage between CS and the
   intergovernmental Bureau for procedural and
   technical issues only.

Regards,
Violet

Proposal-making strategies are definitely different between
low- and high-context participants. Low-context participants
prefer to make proposals with a direct approach, such as
in Anita Johnson's message, "Would like to suggest too that
we consider what we envision is Civil Society's role in the
design...." Several variations of this appeared in the emails
in terms of the manner and approaches by which low-
context participants established their positions and reacted
to and deliberated on the proposals. They normally began

the message with a goal statement or an assertion such as "I have some remarks on this text," or "To have at least wireless access is a must, so I hope that the Secretariat will organize it. Otherwise, why bring notebooks at all? please, do something," or "the point is here that the understanding of ICANN has changed over the years." They did not waste their time in providing a context. They emphasized the articulated goals of what they wanted to propose. Hence, their proposals and responses were usually very specific yet concise and, at other times, lengthy and detailed with clear purposes. For example, Allan voiced his opinion clearly such as, "The paragraph should be deleted. ICANN is far from perfect. Its policy making structures are not as open as we would like..."

Additionally, there was evidence of divergent ways of throwing questions in the email between high and low context. Low-context people question with a more aggressive tone, whereas high-context people's questioning strategy focuses more on seeking for approval or concealing their real intentions. In the following excerpt from James, he responded to a proposal by aggressively illustrating his individuality and made clear that he was not supportive of the proposal regarding "multiple root servers."

> Dear Albert,
> I agree with your email below—phrases like "multiple root servers," "strict international regulation" a extreme for me. By now, Benjamin has sent out the final document. Have you seen it? Will—endorse it? This document is a recommendation to the governments on what should be included in the Plan of Action and Declaration. Has there been any talk about a civil society document? You know that if the governments cannot get their act together, civil society could come through by producing their own declaration and/or plan of action, which may even have the ability to acquire individual government

endorsements. Not sure where this idea is in the
pipeline? Perhaps talk for after Paris—PrepCom3.
James

It was evident that when low-context participants made
proposals, the suggestions were based on an individual
opinion, and they oftentimes requested that an action
be taken, which demonstrated their tendency to be task
oriented.

Hi to the C&T Group and Plenary Groups
The following are some ideas floating around the
Bureau.
I think there should be joint discussions on this
and other questions of common concern, so I am
circulating to these lists (there are no contentious
personal views, I hope). It concerns guidelines for
the allocation of speaker slots at the PrepComs
etc. There is a proposal from Vince Markow (at the
bottom), followed by a comment from James, then
myself (with comments from Vince in there).
But I also think it raises the issue of communication between the Bureau, the C&T Group and the
Plenary Group, and how we make decisions that
affect us all. And the role of the Plenary, in terms of
consulting and approving. Perhaps the C&T Groups
would have proposals to put forward? And the
Plenary?
Steven

The low-context people responded to proposals using a
straight-out approach, with much less effort on obscuring their
emotions. They would also assert their individual views—
sometimes with tactfulness, but many times with aggressive-
ness. For example, when Wutz claimed his authority, he did it

with a slight tone of compromise (see the underlined portion of the message),

> I (wutz) am the main responsible person for the final language of the governance paragraph. I tried to bring all discussed positions on a extrem complex issue into some simple key points. This simplification opens unfortunately the door for misinterpretation. <u>The points you have raised are not in contradiction with the proposed language and I see no basic problem, to harmonize the two approaches</u> (see my comments below).

But later, in his message, he began to apply a more aggressive tone by using capital letters to make his point.

> The proposed paragraph does NOT say that the rules should be different from "common rule of law." In contrary, it says that CS should be in favour of "the common rules of law" for the cyberspace. And even more, in cases, where new or revised or enlarged rules are needed (eCommerce, IPR, InfoSec/Privacy etc.), citizens should be involved directly in the policy development and the rule making.

Another example is a message from Vince that straightforwardly asserts his individual view but is not as harshly presented ("it's not the best but...").

> this is my personal opinion.
>   it's not the best, but
>
>   a. there is no better created (and hence the governments will take immediate control)
>   b. if there is no ICANN, for sure the control over domain and numbers will not by a miracle go

to the Civil Society or the privacy groups, or the scientists; it will go to the governments. And there isn't anything worse than that as of today.

Vince

A fourth example, from Rolf, is more honestly and bluntly expressed. Some might interpret it as rude or offensive, particularly high-context participants who seldom use such direct words as those underlined as follows. As a result, a message like this might intimidate them into not making a counterresponse.

Hi all,
I totally agree with Steven's five points.
Not in the sense of "I like his ideas" but as "That's how it is. Period."
Of course_there is such a thing as the CS plenary which was accepted by a great majority as the final decision making body of CS activities.
> I am seeking support for the above five points from those on this list as I believe we cannot be continually reinventing the past and must move forward. Yes to this also.
I don't understand how these things can come up not even a week after Paris. And I hope we can really move forward and get rid of this discussion soon. I'd rather discuss what we could do better instead of clarifying what has been.
Best, Rolf

Aside from being succinct and concise when proposing or suggesting ideas, low-context people were also capable of sending lengthy messages that detailed their emotions (i.e., anger, frustrations, or disappointments) when they reacted to the proposals that were made by others. They first stated clearly what and how they felt and then provided the context and justification for their feelings or beliefs. This contrasts with high-context participants who first provided the context, with their intentions buried later in the email. In essence, low-context behavior exhibited clear goals, whereas high-context behavior buried their goals.

Dear Mr. Verner Vinson,
I do not speak on matters of substance as the "Focal Point" of the "Media Family." Any suggestion that I did so is inaccurate.

I am also chairman of the Media Caucus, made up of the journalistic organizations attending its meetings and open to all interested related groups attending the Prepcoms and the intersession meeting. Anything I might possibly have reported as being an opinion of the Caucus would have reflected the overwhelming opinion of those taking part in its meetings.

That does not mean that I have given up the right to hold and express my own views, which, I think, are clearly understood as such, when I speak I on my own name.

As for community media, which I highly favor, I assume them to be as diverse and pluralistic as any other media. I rather doubt that they could all or mostly fit your description of their characteristics— unless you mean to say that local media that don't fit that description could not, by definition, be community media, properly so-called. If that were so, it would raise a number of rather intriguing questions. But I am confident in doubting that to be your meaning.

Incidentally, my first paid journalism job nearly 50 years ago was as a jack-of-all-trades at a community weekly newspaper in southern Ohio. It gave me experience as a reporter, editorialist, classified ad taker, proof reader, linotypist and operator of a mid-19th Century flatbed press. So I am an old community newspaperman myself.

In fact, our publisher/editor was a member of the American Socialist Party and his No. 2 was a Quaker and conscientious objector (which I also was at the time), but the newspaper served the whole community and did not attempt to sell an "agenda" based on the views of the staff leaders, even if the editorials—strictly separated from the news—did reflect their sensitivities. The paper won numerous awards as a model community newspaper in the Middle Western region.

The expression "something called community media" was simply meant to convey the idea that there are other possible definitions of what constitutes community written and broadcast press than the cause-oriented one(s) I have encountered in the Civil Society discussions surrounding the WSIS.
Best regards,
Rolan Kiefer

Low-context participants did not hesitate to reveal their personal views, as well as to state with whom they disagreed. Oftentimes, this may be interpreted as an insensitive approach, but low-context people are expressive and true to their intentions. They are willing to self-disclose what they feel rather than hiding it, unlike high-context participants who are more hesitant and careful with self-disclosure. For example, Verner (as follows) states that he was not comfortable with Steven's proposal. The tone of the email is quite forceful. Even though he did compliment Steven's proposal, he directly addressed several other people—Samuel, Wutz, and the Bureau—without concealing his opinions about them. And he ended his email with another forceful question. This is a very different approach from that of a high-context member who would respond just the opposite: providing complimentary statements and/or gratitude, and only then disagreeing, and closing with some polite gestures.

> The problem with the proposal of Steven, which at first sight I applauded because of his positive and constructive approach, is a logical one: who decides and with which representativity who are composing and which competences will have this Task Force? who will give legitimacy to its decisions?
>
> In other words, whatever excelent proposal would result from this Task Force, it will allways be very relative. "Civil Society" is in the first place-still-more a (sociological, political, ideological) concept, then a organizative well defined structure. From this point of view, the concept will be permanently open to multiple interpretations, from a huge variety of legitimate interests. That is at the same time it's force, because everybody has the absolute right to participate.
>
> I agree to maintain Wutz resume as good starting points, because it reinforces this last idea (absolute right to participate) and builds upon the advances made.
>
> I would like to ask the members of the Buro to submit themselves to the practices constructed in this Summit Process. Otherwise they'll loose legitimacy.
> Verner
> P.D. On the Latin American List came up an interesting question: who named the members of the Buro?

Another important characteristic of low-context responses is that, although, generally, their emails are direct and concise, they also exemplify some sense of professionalism and objectivity. The characteristic quality of their responses is that the intention and purpose of the email are clearly stated. For example, Rolf began his email with a friendly note, briefly reflecting his personal view, and then straight away, in one sentence (bolded as follows), clearly stated the goal of his response.

> Hi all,
> It was good to see many of you in Paris, and I think in the end we can be quite satisfied with what we did. Of course, as usual we could do better, especially with more coordination of our activities, a bit more transparency and better pooling of ressources. **This is an attempt to kick off a discussion on CS coordination at PrepCom 3, which will also help for the same task at the summit itself.**
> By this I mean the "inside" activities like monitoring, lobbying, content and themes drafting, press work etc. The "outside" and "half in, half out" activities like the Polymedia Lab or the World Forum on Communication Rights are already being organized in other spaces.
> It is not about content, but about how to structure all our work in order to be more effective and keep everybody better informed on what is going on. This should help us enable better and more equal participation of the whole civil society (on location and elsewhere), make better use of our ressources, and in the end have a bigger impact on the summit outcomes.
> We should prepare well in advance, that is why I suggest to start this discussion now. There are already some deadlines, e.g. Linda from the CS secretariat at ITU wants to have a list of what we need from them at PrepCom3 by this week. And the impressions from Paris are still fresh, so we can better think of what went well and what could be improved.
> *** Where to discuss this?
> In order to not generate another "Spam" problem on this plenary list, I suggest that we set up another

list, coordination@wsis-cs.org, and discuss the details there. Kathryn: Can you do this? (BTW: Kathryn and others did a great job coordinating in Paris!)

I am looking forward to see your ideas and enthusiasm in helping to get this going.
All the best,
Rolf

Findings showed that the proposals that received favorable responses came from both cultural orientations. For example, on the low-context end of the spectrum, Steven's proposals were often clear, direct, and detailed, and, as a result, succeeded in generating numerous positive responses. So did Wutz, Vince, and Rolf when they stated their positions in aggressive proposals. As long as the arguments were sensible, valid, and logical, people seemed to react and respond positively. On the other end of the spectrum, Mariette's lengthy high-context messages that explained her position in a very tactful manner also received favorable responses. Her style was convincing as she used more persuasive tactics. On a similar vein, Rince would often produce a friendly yet convincing message when he proposed something. His name was, in fact, mentioned and referred to many times in the listserv, which points out how influential he is. In essence, much like the problem identification stage, the proposal stage not only required substantive or quality messages, but the manner in which the message was presented also makes a difference.

References

Adler, N.J. 1997. *International Dimensions of Organizational Behavior*, 3rd ed. Cincinnati, OH: South-Western.
Kingdon, J.W. 1995. *Agendas, Alternatives, and Public Policies.* New York: Addison-Wesley Longman.

Chapter 10

Solution

Introduction

For Civil Society, the last stage of decision-making process that the global virtual teams (GVTs) are involved within the WSIS is called *solution*. Adler (1997) and Kingdon (1995) called this stage *choice*. In Figure 10.1, the activities were concentrated in months such as July (n = 18), November (n = 34), and December (n = 28). These three months had 67% of solutions generated, a total of 80, and signify fruitful and successful efforts in arriving at a decision, as well as receiving responses about the solution in the form of alternative solutions. In particular, the Civil Society participants during this period were working toward nominating speakers for the summit and finalizing the language for the documents, decisions that all required endorsements, and consensus.

Once most of the Civil Society participants came forward to endorse a draft document, a consensual decision could be reached about the language of the document. There were several levels of consensus building. On the one hand, Civil

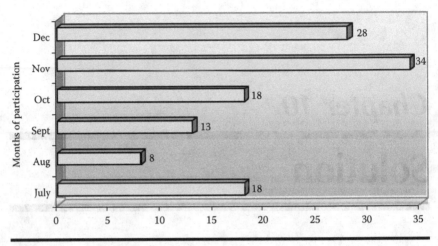

Figure 10.1 Solution activities in WSIS Geneva.

Society participants totally agreed with the language of the document and thus enthusiastically endorsed the document:

> a. Thanks everyone who supported construction of this document. It is constructive, positive and diplomatic but clear! _* endorses it! Good luck in Paris!
> b. Please include the endorsement of _ Venezuela. Thanks.

On the other hand, some people sent an endorsement with reservations:

> a. Dear Benjamin,
>   I can endorse the final version (still with some reservations) concerning the ICT Governance para: -() on behalf of the following institutions:
>
> ■ Global Society Dialogue
> ■ Global Contract Foundation
> ■ International Association for Media and Communication Research

---

* In order to protect confidentiality, the names of the organizations were stripped off from the message even though data were taken from the public archive.

I am accredited under "_". That is, when you
collect primarily "registered" observers, you can
add also "_"

Best wishes, thanks and admiration for the
work and see you Tuesday.

Wutz

At other times, people could not endorse a document
because they disagreed so strongly with the language:

a. All, Participants agreed to remove the last
paragraph of the Governance section. The latest
document is attached, without endorsements.

b. Dear Sandra and Benjamin,
_ cannot endorse the document entitled "Civil
Society Priorities Document" even under its
last issue (07.12.03) for several obvious presentation and content reasons. It's a pity for that
good and intensive job done (mainly by your-
self and Sandra I suppose), which I recognize
and therefore thank both of you. Nevertheless,
I'm sure we could reach an agreement if our
main contribution is taken in account for a
further final issue of that kind of document.
Unfortunately neither of you will attend the
Paris Meeting, and as for me, I can't be present at the first day. But I'll continue as usually
my job in the CS CT working group during
the three days left in order to re-integrate into
the Action Plan these goals _ considers as its
main ones, namely for bridging the N/S communication divide.

This final stage was the most challenging because consensus did not often mean unanimous decisions. In fact, the
participants debated this issue in the listserv that revealed that

there was a misconception among them on the meaning of consensus. As one of the participants clearly stated,

> First, just to say that consensus is not synonymous with unanimity: it means that in the spirit of achieving a common position, there are no overriding objections. However, concerning your point, it has been clear from the outset that documents produced by the Content and Themes group express the consensus of those who sign them and not an overall consensus of Civil Society organizations attending the WSIS.

In other situations, Civil Society participants failed to achieve a solution because the problem was beyond the participants' control or capacity to solve (for example, a problem with infrastructure). These kinds of problems had to be taken up by a higher authority, for example, the bureau or secretariat.

Finally, only in rare instances, the solution was achieved without going through the typical stages because some of participants voluntarily and unilaterally created a solution to the problem:

> Dear Friends,
> As you know the WSIS intersessional is only days away, from July 15–18 at UNESCO headquarters in Paris, France.
> This communication is to inform you that Timothy Rhodes and Rince Plum will be working with the Conference of NGOs in Consultative Status with _ (CONGO) during the intersessional meeting in Paris to report and analyze the negotiations as they are happening. News, reports, and links to relevant Civil Society documents will be provided at: http://www .prepcom.net/wsis. (This site will go live late tomorrow, Tuesday, July 8, if you want a preview.)

We know that many groups are not able to send representatives to the intersessional meeting. We are committed to providing you as much information and news as possible on how the negotiations are proceeding, as well as providing a website where your views, proposals and papers can be shared. Please send any relevant documents to us at timothy.rhodes@ngocongo.org or rince.plum@ngo congo.org and we will see that they are uploaded to the site. During the intersessional, Rince Plum can also be reached at his French mobile number: +36-1254-56-7342.

If you are planning on being at the Intersessional and can volunteer to take notes for a particular session, that would be very appreciated, particularly if you can write in French or Spanish.

So be sure and bookmark www.prepcom.net/wsis and check back every day!
In Peace,
Timothy Rhodes   Rince Plum
timothy.rhodes@ngocongo.org rince.plum@ngocongo
.org

The next section provides analytical descriptions of the decision-making processes through verbatim examples from the archival email messages.

Solution Behaviors

In this stage of the decision-making process, the findings showed that Civil Society participants had contradicting strategies for reaching consensus, finding solutions, and presenting their final decisions. High-context participants presented their decisions in a courteous and appreciative manner. They normally began their email with a friendly or formal acknowledgment. Then, in the first paragraph, it was a common practice for them to first provide the context in which the decisions were made, followed by an expression of gratitude. In the subsequent paragraph(s), the decision was presented and followed by an apology. This strategy is common in group decision making. As an example, the following email from Sandra Burkasa used a collective voice when presenting the final decision and acknowledged and thanked the collective efforts in compiling the document.

> Friends,
> Under the most impossible conditions and with very little time for consultation we have sent the following letter and adjoined compilation text (English only, as you can imagine) to Mr. Sukanessi. Thanks to all who made input.
>   Those comments received today could only be included if they were short and simple and not contradictory with other proposals. I am sorry there wasn't time to process it all. We can continue work on this for the November meeting.
> Sandra Burkasa

Quite the opposite tone is taken by low-context participants who commonly used direct and precise statements to inform other participants of the decisions made—for instance, Wutz's endorsement, "Here I fully agree. This is a "friendly amendment" and "I would fully endorse the references...", or the announcement from Venda Busara:

> Hi Victor,
> I have just received a notification that there is not room available for the LAC caucus from 8–9 am. They are proposing us to have a room from 9 to 10. Please, reply to the message I have sent to the

> LAC caucus members who will be attending the
> PrepCom3 to decide collectively what to do.
> Thanks!
> Venda

Low-context participants would directly state their decision
first, and then provide any remaining suggestions but only if
the suggestions would not change their decision. In Sandra's
email quoted earlier in this section, she discusses the process that they went through in arriving at the final document,
whereas Rolf (as follows) is concerned with presenting the
final product itself. Note the different communication styles
and tone. Rolf's intention was to explicitly announce that the
document was ready and that the participants could read it.

> Hi all,
> The Civil Society comments to the non-paper and
> the accompanying letter from Sandra are now online
> at http://www.worldsummit2003.org. There you also
> find a direct link to the non-paper and a new article
> on the process that has been going on in Geneva
> since PrepCom3.
> Direct link to the comments for you references:
> <http://www.worldsummit2003.de/download_en
> /comments-on-nonpaper-30-10-2003-final.rtf>
> Best, Rolf

Both Venda and Rolf made a decision that is based on
self-interest and took action when it was appropriate without
further consultation from the group. The findings showed
that, in many cases, this approach or strategy was much more
effective when there was a prominent leadership role that
is played by a specific individual. For example, there was a
discussion on the problems of infrastructure such as wireless
connections, logistics, and Internet services. Renee immediately reacted to the problems that people faced by posting a

brief and meaningful email that said, "I will further negotiate tomorrow morning." She then promptly followed up with a message that outlined a solution:

> Dear Sandra and all,
> After some discussion and negotiations, the situation for meeting and work rooms is as follows:
>
> > One large room (9) for CS next to the Conference rooms, smaller rooms (14) (15) (16) in the adjacent building for CSB and other meetings and (A 12, seating 12–15) for the drafting persons or CTGroup.
> > Internet Cafe with 10–15 connected computers, will also be available.
>
> Renee

In fact, an analysis of the distribution of Renee's participation across the stages of the decision-making process showed that she contributed more in the proposal-making and solution stage, rather than the problem identification stage.

Another example is Raymond's solution to the *accreditation* issue for the Civil Society organizations. He provided detailed and clear instructions, and his communication style was direct. He also provided details on where he got the information so that his information was substantiated and could be independently verified by others if they chose to do so.

> Hi,
> Raymond Jacob here, in Minneapolis for two weeks.
> In checking on accreditation for another organization, I went to the www.itu.int site and clicked on the red "accreditatin" word on the right.
> A page appears in the center of which are two lines, the second of which says "list of entitites that have requested accreditation."

Click on that and there is a list of almost 2000 organizations. I went to our organization, Intl. Council for Caring Communities, clicked on it to see our web site, and came up with Indo-Canadian Chamber of Commerce, another "ICCC" as is our organization.

I suggest that you all check if the web site that is associated with your organization really is yours!
Raymond J.

In conclusion, the way team members negotiate a decision to reach a solution is all dependent on the culturally laden values as rooted in the team members' communicative behaviors. Apparently, the high-context members seemed to have a more courteous manner of presenting their decisions as they took time to present their solutions. For instance, members would provide subtle statements in the opening line of their communications, afterwards, leading members to their final decisions. On the other hand, the low-context members prefer to state their decisions clearly and quickly without delay, and they state it in a straightforward fashion by being transparent about their feelings and thoughts about such a solution. These two strategies of reaching to a solution need to be well recognized by GVT leaders and members because such contradictory approaches can create miscommunication, misinterpretations, frustrations, and conflicts if members do not handle such challenges with care and tact.

References

Adler, N.J. 1997. *International Dimensions of Organizational Behavior*, 3rd ed. Cincinnati, OH: South-Western.

Kingdon, J.W. 1995. *Agendas, Alternatives, and Public Policies*. New York: Addison-Wesley Longman.

CULTURAL INFLUENCES ON DISTRIBUTED DECISION MAKING

IV

We need a plan; so, let's be straightforward!

Dr. Hannah Barak, a medical officer in Baghdad Hospital, was taken aback this morning. Her colleague, Dr. David Soltes, refused to agree with her suggestions on how to carry out some complex procedures in an upcoming surgery. When they spoke over Skype, he bluntly said that he would do it a certain way based on his many years of experience in Slovakia. Hannah was not upset by his decision, but she was disturbed by the way that he had been communicating his ideas through virtual communication for the past few months. He was firm, direct, and precise and allowed little or no negotiation. His emails were short and composed largely of "what needs to be done—plans." Hannah, however, strongly believes that, in every situation, matters need to be carefully discussed and negotiated. She prefers a strategy that is based on a sort of haggling in which the conversation is steered toward a *win–win* rather than a *win–lose* outcome. Using such a strategy, a relationship can be developed, and, gradually, trust will form. Dr. Soltes, on the other hand, felt that there was nothing much to discuss. As a well-known eye specialist who would be flown over to Baghdad next week, he is entrusted with a crucial task. What matters to him is to thus execute that task as efficiently as possible. His belief is that a successful completion of the task comes first, and then trust follows.

Chapter 11

Online Communicative Behaviors Based on Cultural Variations

Introduction

Fundamentally, people exhibit different choices, styles, and strategies in decision making based on their culture; these differences are particularly striking between high- and low-context communication styles. The general difference in decision strategy is between detailed and agreed-upon decisions versus shallow information exchanges. Adler (1997) also examined other decision-making issues, such as whether decisions are made quickly or slowly and whether information and alternatives are discussed sequentially or holistically. These different approaches appear in various locations along the high-context/low-context continuum. Therefore, the main purpose of this chapter is to provide a brief and broad understanding on the following research question:

> Are there discernible patterns of cultural variations
> evident in the email messages that were exchanged

among the Civil Society GVT members? If so, is Hall's high-context versus low-context dimension sufficient to explain these variations?

Results are presented based on the cultural dimension of context: high context and low context. For each end of the spectrum, the findings are further analyzed based on two variables: (1) intercultural communication style and (2) cultural values, which will be presented in Chapters 12 and 13. Specifically, for high-context participants, intercultural communication styles were analyzed based on constructs like indirectness and ambiguity, while cultural values were analyzed based on collectivism versus relationship oriented. For low-context participants, intercultural communication styles were analyzed based on constructs like direct and detail oriented, while cultural values were looked at in terms of individualism and task oriented (see Figure 11.1).

The findings from this study clearly show that there are discernible patterns of culture based on high- and low-context

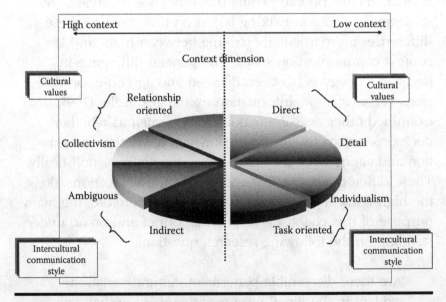

Figure 11.1   Context cultural dimension.

orientation. These cultural variations were evident in the messages that were posted by Civil Society participants when they engaged in decision-making activities. The overall proportion of high- and low-context behaviors (see Figure 11.2) were strikingly different with 68% of the instances representing low-context behaviors (n = 2,047) and only 32% representing high-context behaviors (n = 980).

As shown in Figure 11.3, further analysis revealed more instances of intercultural communication styles (52% of total

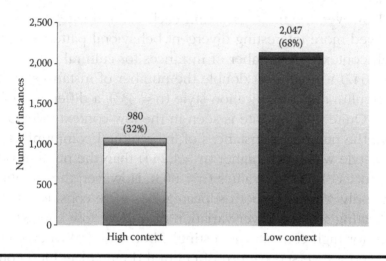

Figure 11.2 Proportion of high-context versus low-context messages.

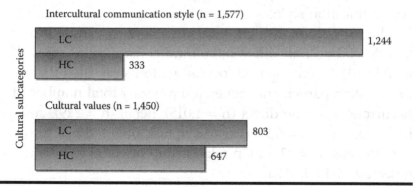

Figure 11.3 Cultural subcategories: intercultural communication style versus cultural values.

occurrences, n = 1,577) than of cultural values (48%, n = 1,450). Analyzing across cultural categories, a significant behavioral pattern was observed in the high- and low-context participants' intercultural communication styles. Low-context communication style accounted for 79% (n = 1,244) compared to high context, which accounted for only 21% (n = 333). For cultural values, there was much less variation between the two cultural categories: low-context behaviors accounted for 55% (n = 803), while high-context behaviors accounted for 45% (n = 647).

However, the findings within each cultural category showed more interesting divergent behavioral patterns. For high context, the number of instances for cultural values (n = 647) were almost double the number of instances of intercultural communication style (n = 333), a difference of 51%. Quite the opposite is seen in the low-context orientation: the number of instances of intercultural communication style was much higher (n = 1,244) than the number of instances of cultural values (n = 803). However, the variation was only 35% when both subcategories were considered, indicating a much lower variation overall for low context than for high context. Interestingly, both cultural categories showed a reversed pattern of cultural dominance: high context had a higher correspondence with cultural values, and low context had a higher correspondence with intercultural communication style.

The proportion of high versus low context can be broken down into four different cultural constructs, as shown in Table 11.1. Although the overall patterns revealed that low-context participants generated a higher total number of occurrences for the direct (n = 1,015), detail (n = 229), and individualistic (n = 628) constructs, task oriented had fewer occurrences (n = 175) than relationship oriented (n = 245), as reflected in Table 11.1.

Furthermore, as shown in Figure 11.4, a comparison was made across constructs; the shaded area points out

Table 11.1 Overall Distribution of High- versus Low-Context Cultural Constructs

Cultural Subcategories	High Context	Instances	Low Context	Instances	Total
Intercultural communication style	Indirect	287 (29%)	Direct	1,015 (50%)	1,302
	Ambiguous	46 (5%)	Detail oriented	229 (11%)	275
	Collectivistic	402 (41%)	Individualistic	628 (31%)	1,030
Cultural values	Relationship oriented	245 (25%)	Task oriented	175 (9%)	420
Total		980 (100%)		2,047 (101%)[a]	3,300

[a] Total percentage does not equal 100% due to rounding.

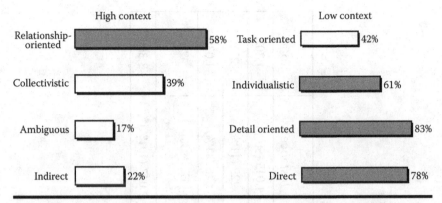

Figure 11.4 Comparison of cultural constructs for high and low context.

the constructs that generated a higher percentage when compared in terms of high context versus low context. This analysis shows that, for high context, the relationship-oriented construct was higher, accounting for 58%, compared to task oriented, which accounted for 42% of total occurrences. The other three constructs for low context showed higher percentages than their high-context counterparts. However, what stood out in the finding is that from the low-context constructs called *detail* and *direct*. The detail construct was represented by 83% of total occurrences, while only a mere 17% was represented by the *ambiguous* construct from high context. Likewise, for direct, the total occurrences for low context were significantly higher (78%) than the construct of *indirect* for high context (only 22% of total occurrences). In essence, for the parallel comparison, the dominant construct for high context is relationship oriented, while, for low context, the dominant construct was detail and direct communication style.

The following section expands on each of the cultural context orientations by detailing which cultural construct is more dominant.

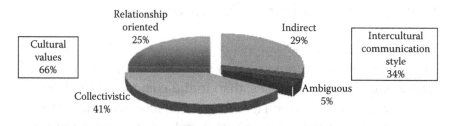

Figure 11.5 **Proportion of cultural constructs observed for high-context orientation.**

High-Context Cultural Orientation

For the high-context cultural orientation,* collectivistic features were seen in 41% of total occurrences (see Figure 11.5). The next most prominent cultural values, indirect and relationship oriented, were seen in 29% and 25% of occurrences, respectively. In combination, these two constructs made up 54% of the total occurrences. Despite the low percentage of relationship-oriented occurrences compared to the other two high-context constructs, its occurrence was still much higher than its opposite (task oriented). Ambiguous was the least significant construct, appearing in only 5% of the voluminous number of email messages.

For high-context cultural orientation, the dominant cultural patterns exhibited were in the cultural values, which totaled 66%. On the other hand, the two types of intercultural communication style (indirect and ambiguous) accounted for only 34% of the total high-context occurrences. In addition, indirectness and ambiguity messages (n = 333) together accounted for only 11% of all cultural occurrences (n = 3,027).

---

* The analysis was made *within* the high-context category, i.e., between direct and ambiguous, or between collectivistic and relationship oriented. The comparison made in the "Introduction" section (see Figure 11.3) was done *across* categories, i.e., high versus low context, relationship oriented versus task oriented.

Low-Context Cultural Orientation

Results showed that low-context behaviors were reflected more in the intercultural communication style subcategory, with 60% of total low-context occurrences, than in the cultural values subcategory, with only 40% (see Figure 11.6). Notably, under the subcategory of intercultural communication style, direct accounted for 82% of the combined construct, while detail accounted for only 18%. This strongly suggests that directness is the main characteristic of low-context communications. For cultural values, individualism represented 31% of total occurrences and task oriented only 9%, indicating that individualism was the next most prominent cultural characteristic of low-context communications.

Based on the findings of GVTs in Civil Society, it could be deduced that, with cultural knowledge, organizations can identify how people initially learn to communicate given these context-based considerations: what to say (choice of words), to whom to utter such words (what the relationship is between the sender of the message and the recipient), why use such words (reasons and justifications for communicating), when it is best to be *said* (the timing and location of communication), and, finally, in which manner it is best said (the approaches

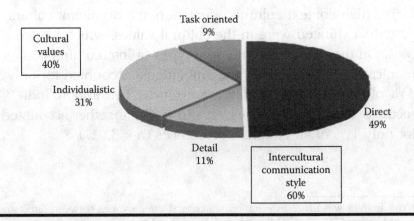

Figure 11.6 Proportion of cultural constructs observed for low-context orientation.

used). On the other end of the cultural spectrum, *content* has a bearing on communication because words are sought after, and not *context*. Such culturally attuned challenges need to be learned and dealt with in the GVT context. Chapters 12 and 13 provide an in-depth description of the patterns of behaviors that are exhibited in each subcategory: intercultural communication styles and cultural values. Furthermore, each of the subcategories will be explained in terms of the cultural patterns of behaviors and supported by verbatim examples from the email messages.

Reference

Adler, N.J. 1997. *International Dimensions of Organizational Behavior*, 3rd ed. Cincinnati, OH: South-Western.

Chapter 12

Intercultural Communication Styles

Introduction

Based on the concept of *context*, Hall explained that, in a high-context (HC) culture, people usually establish their communication styles dependent on contextual factors such as what, why, when, who, and how to communicate with another person. Yet, in a low-context (LC) culture, one's communication styles are independent of contextual factors, as mentioned earlier in this section. Instead, it is dependent on a content-based factor in which *words* that are either verbally said or written are considered significant when collaborating with others such as in the global virtual team (GVT) work structure (Zakaria et al. 2012). If that is the case, people and organizations need to explore the impact of culture on one's communicative behaviors.

In order to avoid misunderstanding and misinterpretation, it is important to comprehend the meaning in what a person says and how things are said—i.e., the communication style that one uses for generating ideas, exchanging opinions, sharing knowledge, and expressing ideas. In a similar vein, the way people arrive at a decision varies significantly from one culture to another since conflict is viewed differently based on the cultural context. Cultural differences may also impact the decision-making process, with individuals from LC cultures responding in a direct, confrontational way and expecting quick answers, whereas HC participants respond in an evasive and nonconfrontational manner, leading to an indirect, less active approach to resolution. Thus, the discussions in the following sections will detail out the distinctive differences between HC and LC communication styles.

Intercultural Communication Style: Indirect versus Direct

According to Hall (1976), he predicted that people from HC cultures would generally use an indirect style of communication. People in HC cultures are also more likely to be silent about their feelings and thoughts (Hall 1976). For HC people, one must *read between the lines* in order to understand the true meaning of a message (Deresky 2000). The concept of *saving face*, examined by Ting-Toomey (1999), theorizes that HC people are often cautious or ambiguous in their speech out of a desire to avoid causing embarrassment or humiliation to others. In this type of culture, conflicts are avoided at any cost. Conversely, LC participants expressed their opinions and intentions more freely and more often said exactly what they meant and what they wanted people to understand. They expressed themselves in a more explicit manner that supplied all the situational elements that are needed to understand their message (Hall 1976). In an LC culture, individuals tend to convey important messages through the use of explicit verbal codes.

HC people approach decision making holistically. The process requires complete information and a discussion of all the alternatives before making a decision (Takayama 1972).

Because of this elaborative discussion, the decision-making process is slower than for LC people. HC people tend to take their time in thinking through a matter and only then make a decision. They are considered *be-ers*, a culture that focuses on *being* (Trompenaars and Hampden-Turner 2000), allowing change to occur at its own slow pace. They do not rush things and view time as generational (Adler 1997). Our study of Civil Society list participants found an evidence of such behavior; for example, when arriving at a decision, HC participants used phrases like "after thinking about this…" showing that they have given their decision some thought and that their decision was made based on all considerations. In messages written using an HC communication style, "…information is less contextual, with less detail, more general references to the overall situation, and often more politeness strategies" (Thomas 1998, p. 13). LC participants, on the other hand, would straight away inform of their decision, and no indication was given of how long they considered the matter or how they arrived at a decision.

HC people also tend to remain silent in meetings; as a result, they are often very good observers and listeners. LC people, on the other hand, prefer to discuss alternatives in a preplanned sequence and make incremental decisions for each alternative that is discussed. They desire quick decisions, so attending a meeting with LC people means jumping into the matter right away. (Trompenaars' metaphor for HC is the *chief listener*, while, for LC, it is the *dauntless decision maker*.)

Again, our Civil Society study found evidence of such behavior; in one particular incident, an LC Civil Society member jumped into a discussion and said, "I think that this issue is raging on and on. I know that people need to have the opportunity to choose and express opinions. I think that there also comes a time when the additions have to stop and we have to look at the list we have and choose," and then went on to state what they thought is needed to be done.

LC people are apt to keep their focus on the agenda and get frustrated if the agenda is abandoned during a meeting, in contrast to meetings among HC people where matters may be repeatedly revisited or remain unresolved. According to Trompenaars and Hampden-Turner (2000), LC people are the *do-ers*, action oriented and focused on *doing*, who believe that setting agendas can help them be more focused. LC people typically have plans carefully outlined, with specific deadlines and required progress reports. The exception to this is that, sometimes, LC people may prefer to have shallow information exchanges prior to a meeting so that, during the meeting, they can focus on making decisions and can exchange ideas, express opinions, and state their positions by presenting their arguments.

Bresnahan et al. (2002) also noted that HC communication styles use a nonassertive approach; they place less value on talk and emphasize more on the nonverbal aspects when presenting their ideas. Messages are sent in a subtle manner wherein the meanings are buried in their nonverbal cues as they tend to rely on fewer words—making it hard to comprehend or interpret its meanings. On the other hand, LC communication styles are direct and assertive as they value straightforward talk. Following from that, Bresnahan et al. observed that HC communication styles have two different underlying assumptions. When a communication takes place with the in-group* members, there is a shared understanding among the members.

The form of a message that HC individuals send to the in-group members is thus terse, containing restricted codes (Gudykunst et al. 1996). Restricted code means that a message does not contain verbose words; rather, the message is composed using shortened words, phrases, and sentences (like a

---

* In-group is a term that is used to signify a group of people with whom a person is familiar and has a strong relational bond. The in-group is considered the *trusted* group, and its members are often spouse, family, and close friends (Triandis 1988).

secret code). The messages rely more on nonverbal elements such as tone of the message, the nature of relationship, social context, and the use of silence. Only the receiver or possibly another in-group member would be successful in decoding or interpreting the meaning of the message.

Similarly, when an HC communication takes place with an out-group* member with whom the message sender has no strong or prior relationship (for example, an acquaintance or a stranger), an individual does not usually provide a lot of personal information; his or her message is written at a superficial level, again producing a short message where no details are included. Because of this, the stranger receiving the message may have difficulty interpreting the message. Also, openness is not a key characteristic of HC communication. As such, an HC individual rarely discloses a large amount of personal information (Gudykunst & Kim 2002) to strangers. On the other hand, group-based information such as group memberships, status, and background are likely to be disclosed in such conversations (Gudykunst & Nishida 1986). Both assumptions mentioned earlier in this section explain the terse and short messages that are used in the HC communication style, whether written or spoken.

HC participants were not comfortable expressing their concerns forthrightly, which made their emails longer than those of LC participants. The participants had to read such email closely in order to understand the main concerns. Sometimes, a message contained many concerns, and, as a consequence, the messages failed to address the main, urgent problems that required actions or solutions.

---

* Out-group members, on the other hand, are people to whom a person is not close to or known of, whom they considered as their acquaintance or total strangers (Triandis 1988). The Japanese society often used a term called *one of us* or *one of them* to signify the distinction between in-group and out-group members (Ferraro 1998). This form of distinction also determines which conversational greeting will be used.

Intercultural Communication Style: Ambiguous versus Detailed

In some other situations, during the WSIS participation, HC people do produce messages that are lengthy, inexact, and ambiguous. This is strongly evident in situations where an individual wants to avoid telling the truth about some situation for the fear of hurting someone's feelings, embarrassing a person or himself or herself, or confronting a conflicting situation (Ferraro 2003; LeBaron 2003; Ting-Toomey 1999; Hall 1976). The ambiguous style is also used to protect the feelings of people whom an individual is in contact with, especially his or her in-group members or the group that he or she belongs to (Triandis 1994). In such cases, people will camouflage their meaning or bury their true intentions in long-drawn-out messages. HC people are also more comfortable with subtle, uncertain, and qualifier words such as *maybe*, *perhaps*, and *probably* (Okabe 1983, p. 34) embedded in the long texts to avoid giving an assertive or forceful impression to their message receivers. As Hall (1976) says, "...she will talk around and around the point, in effect putting all the pieces in place except the crucial one. Placing it properly—this keystone—is the role of his [or her] interlocutor" (p. 98).

Under some circumstances, HC people often intend to protect the feelings of their in-group members (Triandis 1994), or, when they want to avoid confrontation, they will write long messages, to the point that the messages can be incomprehensible to the LC audience who considers the message to be without substance or quality. But, because of their strong need for a harmonious environment and avoidance of conflict, HC people can also produce extremely effective, diplomatic, and tactful messages through their *politeness* strategy (Ferraro 2003; Okabe 1983).

In contrast, participants from LC cultures are more apt to separate issues from people ("don't take it personally"), whereas the participants from HC cultures are more likely to blend the two and may take personal affront to a professional disagreement. Work and personal issues are integrated, and, thus, oftentimes, work disagreements are perceived as personal conflicts. The consequence for Civil Society participants is that the participants from LC cultures are more apt to view disagreements as an integral part of knowledge sharing—not only acceptable but also even a positive activity that encourages creative discourse—whereas HC participants may perceive open disagreement and confrontation as highly insulting and as causing both parties to lose face (Zakaria et al. 2004; Ting-Toomey 1999).

For the LC communication style, they often presented a detailed message to their members when collaborating. A detailed message contains extensive, elaborate explanations and descriptions and/or is full of instructions, procedures, or steps to be taken on the subject under discussion. Furthermore, the LC communication style—verbal or written—relies on the heavy use of words. Hence, LC communication is content dependent where words are the primary strategy to effective communication (Gudykunst & Kim 2002; Hall 1976). The *conversational maxim* introduced by Grice (1975) offers four elements of social interaction:

1. *Quantity maxim*: The contribution should be as informative as possible.
2. *Quality maxim*: The contribution should be truthful.
3. *Relevancy maxim*: The contribution should be relevant.
4. *Manner maxim*: The contribution should be brief and orderly.

These maxims are applicable to LC communication style (LeBaron 2003; Gudykunst & Kim 2002). Supporting these maxims, Gudykunst and Ting-Toomey (1988) identified four distinct verbal interpersonal communication styles: (1) direct,

(2) elaborated, (3) instrumental, and (4) personal. By integrating Grice's four-point maxim with Gudykunst's four verbal styles, the key aspects of LC communication become the following: (1) LC communication puts the emphasis on directness because LC people believe that information should be straight to the point, and accurate, and that people should not contribute to others more or less information than necessary, (2) LC communication is based on sufficient evidence and facts and is consistent with the participants' feelings (Hall 1976), (3) LC people only contribute information in the context of the conversations, and (4) LC people avoid any ambiguity, excessiveness, and verbosity in their communication.

It is well established that LC people send a short, succinct, and terse message when they express their opinions or state their feelings. LC people value openness. Speaking their minds and telling the truth are some of their key communication characteristics, in unison with the quality maxim. The terse messages are often used in situations when they want to assert a point, without the fear of hurting the feelings of others because they believe in truth (Gudykunst & Nishida 1986; Grice 1975). LC people value individualism and base their behavior on true feelings (Frymier et al. 1990). They are also more inclined to express bluntly and talk freely than HC people. Although the truth might hurt, this strategy is useful in being precise and accurate. Sometimes, HC audience views this strategy as lack of tact or diplomacy; hence, the message is interpreted as harsh, rude, or blunt (Zakaria et al. 2004).

However, in some situations, LC people do send long messages when they communicate, but they do this for different motivations from the HC people. The purpose of sending detailed and accurate information is to provide explanations, support their intention or arguments, and give instructions. LC people are often seen as providing the fine details of a subject matter because they are task-oriented people (Triandis 1994). They base their communication on the task first, and then the relationship; therefore, they provide detailed instructions to explain to people how to proceed with a task. In this case, LC people emphasize the *quantity* maxim, which is to be as informative and resourceful as possible. Conversely, HC people base their communication on relationship-oriented purposes; hence, the long message is written for the purpose to maintain and protect the relationship built.

The differences between the terse and lengthy messages for HC and LC are thus rooted in the motivations of producing such messages, as illustrated in Table 12.1.

As mentioned in the "Introduction" section and under Chapter 5 for Hall theoretical framework, context alludes to what, why, how, when, and to whom a message is sent. In essence, HC communication is *context dependent.* The decision on how much information is disclosed (amount of information, short or long messages) in HC communication depends largely on the receiver of the message (who) and the topic of the message (what is to be disclosed and what is to be kept private or confidential), whereas LC communication is *content dependent,* which places strong emphasis on words, either verbal or written. Establishing common ground between and among Civil Society participants is challenging because it requires that people take the differences in communication styles into consideration in accordance with each member's cultural preferences; only then can participants successfully ground their communication and effectively engage in collaborative efforts or activities.

In conclusion, the study showed that the *direct* communicative behavior belonging to LC cultures had three parts: (1) an assertive statement, followed by (2) a body of text that explains, clarifies, or justifies the assertion, and, finally, (3) a conclusion that wraps up one's view. Whereas, for HC cultures, people not only displayed politeness and tactfulness in their messages but also sometimes apologized excessively—a key sign of not wanting to offend other participants. Sometimes, this causes conflict—at worst, HC cultures may view the straightforward messages and explicit words of LC cultures as attacking, rude, outspoken, or unacceptable.

Table 12.1 Types of Messages Based on HC and LC Dimension: Ambiguous vs. Detail

Length of Written Messages	High Context	Low Context
Short	HC people write *brief* and terse messages because • They expect people to understand and read their intentions, thoughts, or feelings. • They are uncomfortable to disclose their personal information to strangers. • They use short phrases or sentences with uncertain qualifier words such as probably, maybe, and perhaps.	LC people write *succinct* messages because • They communicate in a direct fashion—"out in the open"—so that people understand their intention explicitly. • They are open and frank about what they feel, even to strangers. • They use strong and assertive words like certainly, absolutely, and positively.
Long	HC people write *ambiguous* messages because • They want to mask their intentions and protect oneself and others from being hurt or experiencing embarrassing situations. • They want to ensure their relationship is maintained—focus on relationship orientation.	LC people write *detailed* messages because • They write detailed explanations and instructions for complex task-related information. • They want to ensure people can carry out the task assigned—focus on task orientation.
Emphasis	• Context-dependent	• Content-dependent

References

Adler, N.J. 1997. *International Dimensions of Organizational Behavior*, 3rd ed. Cincinnati, OH: South-Western.

Bresnahan, M.J., Shearman, S.M., Lee, S.Y., Ohashi R. & Mosher, D. 2002. Personal and cultural differences in responding to criticism in three countries. *Asian Journal of Social Psychology*, 5(2), 93–105.

Deresky, H. 2000. *International Management: Managing Across Borders and Cultures*, 3rd ed. Upper Saddle River, NJ: Prentice Hall.

Ferraro, G.P. 2003. *The Cultural Dimension of International Business*. Upper Saddle River, NJ: Prentice Hall.

Frymier, A.B., Klopf, D.W. & Ishii, S. 1990. Japanese and Americans compared on the affect orientation construct. *Psychological Reports*, 66, 985–986.

Grice, H.P. 1975. Logic and conversation. In P. Cole & J.L. Morgan (Eds.), *Speech Acts* (pp. 41–58). New York: Academic Press.

Gudykunst, W.B. & Kim, Y.Y. 2002. *Communicating with Strangers: An Approach to Intercultural Communication*, 4th ed. London: McGraw-Hill.

Gudykunst, W.B. & Nishida, T. 1986. Attributional confidence in low- and high-context cultures. *Human Communication Research*, 12, 525–549.

Gudykunst, W.B. & Ting-Toomey, S. 1988. *Culture and Interpersonal Communication*. Newbury Park, CA: SAGE.

Gudykunst, W.B., Matsumoto, Y., Ting-Toomey, S., Nishida, T., Kim, K. & Heyman, S. 1996. The influence of cultural individualism-collectivism, self-construal, and individual values on communication styles across cultures. *Human Communication Research*, 22(4), 510–543.

Hall, E.T. 1976. *Beyond Culture*. Garden City, NJ: Anchor Books/ Doubleday.

LeBaron, M.L. 2003. *Bridging Cultural Conflicts: New Approaches for a Changing World*. San Francisco: Jossey-Bass Publishers.

Okabe, R. 1983. Cultural assumptions of East and West: Japan and the U.S. In W.B. Gudykunst (Ed.), *Intercultural Communication Theory* (pp. 28–40). Beverly Hills, CA: SAGE.

Takayama, S. 1972. Group decision making in Japanese management. *International Studies of Management and Organization*,
2(2), 183–186.

Thomas, J. 1998. Contexting Koreans: Does the high/low model
work? *Business Communication Quarterly*, 61(4), 9–22.

Ting-Toomey, S. 1999. *Communicating Across Cultures*. New York:
Guilford.

Triandis, H.C. 1994. *Culture and Social Behavior*. New York:
McGraw-Hill.

Triandis, H.C. 1988. Collectivism vs. individualism: A reconceptu-
alization of basic concept in cross-cultural psychology. In G.
Verma & C. Bagley (Eds.), *Cross-Cultural Studies of Personality,
Attitudes, and Cognition* (pp. 60–95). London: Macmillan.

Trompenaars, F. & Hampden-Turner, C. 2000. *Building Cross-
Cultural Competence: How to Create Wealth from Conflicting
Values*. New Haven, CT: Yale University Press.

Zakaria, N., Cogburn, D.L., Khadapkar, P.S. & Lois, C. 2012.
Examining cultural effects on distributed decision-making
processes using keyword analysis and data mining techniques.
International Journal of Business and System Research, 6(3),
313–335.

Zakaria, N., Amelinckx, A. & Wilemon, D. 2004. Working together
apart? Building a knowledge sharing culture for global virtual
teams. *Creativity and Innovation Management*, 13(1), 15–29.

Chapter 13

Cultural Values

Introduction

In the distributed decision-making process, evidently, cultural values play a crucial role in varied forms and manners for global virtual team (GVT) participants. For example, two extremes exist in how different cultures make decisions: (1) a belief that people can make decisions based on *one best way* or (2) a belief that the best way varies and is based on situation. In the latter case, the best way depends on the "values, beliefs, and behavioral patterns of the people involved" (Adler 1997, p. 168). Hall (1976) supports this perspective in his argument concerning context and content. People who place greater emphasis on context make decisions based on affective goals and situation (e.g., where, when, why, and with whom they are dealing) called *relationship orientation*, whereas people who place priority on content depend on instrumental purposes or pragmatic goals called *task orientation* (Zakaria et al. 2003). For this second type of people, decisions are less dependent on situation; rather, they rely more on facts and figures. Therefore, this chapter discusses two aspects of cultural values that are inherent in explaining the decision-making behaviors of GVTs given their cultures: (1) individualistic versus collectivistic and (2) task oriented versus relationship oriented.

Individualism versus Collectivism

In terms of cultural values, the individualism of low-context participants favors accountability, self-opinion, and self-interest. These qualities were given a priority over group-based inter-ests, in contrast with high-context participants. For example, Wutz took the initiative to ensure that Civil Society partici-pants perfectly understood his position:

> Hi Marion,
> I (wutz) am the main responsible person for the
> final language of the governance paragraph. I tried
> to bring all discussed positions on extreme complex
> issue into some simple key points. This simplification
> opens unfortunately the door for misinterpretation.
> The points you have raised are not in contradiction
> with the proposed language and I see no basic prob-
> lem, to harmonize the two approaches.
>   (see my comments below)....

Individualism was also evident when people agreed to take up a task with statements like the following: "I would like to volunteer to assume this role. Please put me down. I would be happy to work on it with someone else" or "I would like to invite you to...," or "I had sent a program and registration form to the plenary. It sits there for approval." All these state-ments highlight the act of *self* and are not in reference to other people or other parties, nor do they allude to collective initia-tives or projects; rather, they focus on a single person.

Aside from the tone of the message being individualistic, the messages exhibit a high usage of singular pronouns such as *I*, *my*, and *your*, as illustrated in this example (emphasis added):

> I like what you have outlined in this email below.
> I think these are three concrete steps that will help
> to bring Civil Society together for probably the most
> important Prepcom of the WSIS process.
>
> I particular like point No. 01 below. I think that
> CS needs to be more active and engaging substan-
> tively on the two main documents of the Summit
> (Declaration and Plan of Action), especially due to
> the fact that the purpose of Prepcom 3 is to complete
> these documents for the Summit in December.
>
> My comment is that perhaps we can have a one-
> two page document ready before Prepcom 3 for all
> of civil society and especially the newcomers (pos-
> sibly could be distributed at the orientation session
> sponsored by CONGO). It would include a list of
> "past caucuses", possible "new caucuses", how to
> schedule meeting space, etc.

For cultural values such as *collectivism*, results showed that high-context participants emphasized the collective voice rather than the individual voice. This was demonstrated by the substantial use of plural pronouns such as *we*, *our*, and *us*. For example, in the following message, the writer used the collec-tive voice throughout.

> Thanks to everyone who has sent in comments on
> the document. We will do our best to incorporate
> the suggested modifications. except, perhaps, any are
> likely to be particularly polemical or that would con-
> siderably lengthen the document. We will consider
> what to do with the proposal on work/employment
> (sent in Spanish). In effect this is an important issue

and maybe we should give it the space even if it means lengthening the document.

With respect to any other issues that are missing and would require more lengthy development, we should remember that there will also be space to address more specific issues in greater detail in specific documents.

We would have liked to get the document out earlier for comment but as much of the caucus input only came in this week it was not possible. So those who have made suggestions for modifications, it would help us if you could send us specific and concise language today. We want to finalize the document by tomorrow to give time to those who prefer to see the final version before endorsing it.

We cannot, of course, expect a consensus document to be perfect for everyone; that is part of the compromise that consensus implies.

Collectivism was also demonstrated by the fact that the interest of the group was much more dominant than self-interest. Many of the messages focused on collective opinions or efforts. For example, this message projects a strongly unified voice from the Civil Society organization as they contest the suggestions that were made by others:

We find the suggestions for regimentation in civil society input to plenary, through the CSB, quite disturbing, especially given the attention that went in to organizing the time slots during the recent Paris meeting. Also disturbing is the undertone of the suggestions by the CSB co-chair, which we interpret as an intent to restrict freedom of expression and an introduction of censorship that is at odds with core CS values. We strongly oppose the attempt to use disagreements in a few caucuses as a pretext for

questioning the legitimacy of the CS plenary as a
whole, and attempting to usurp the responsibility for
content-related issues and concentrating this within
the CSB.

Similarly, this excerpt demonstrates the collective efforts
that were made by the World Forum on Community
Networking:

For our first issue, we have selected about ten civil
society lists, followed their discussions and prepared
summaries that have been translated in order to post
them on our site. This way, we hope to facilitate
exchanges between lists working in French, English
and Spanish and to allow a greater number of people
and organizations to be part of the discussions.

Collectivistic participants would often weave together
serious matters and peripheral issues in their messages.
Sometimes, the message digressed into anecdotal stories, for
example, "We were saddened to hear about the disastrous
earthquake in Iran and the many people who have died. If
there is any way that I can help with regard to mental health
information and services in the wake of disaster, please let me
know." Collectivistic messages were sometimes related to the
main point, other times totally unrelated. Some high-context
participants sent messages asking after the well-being of specific participants or sent helpful messages to provide people
with extra information without even being asked. This behavior suggests that collectivistic participants adopted affective or
expressive goals, whereas individualistic participants favored
instrumental or pragmatic goals.

The findings of our Civil Society study support those of
Mills and Clark (1982) who made the distinction between
communal and exchange relationships. They contend that
individualistic participants often try to maintain a balance

between profit and loss in a relationship. Conversely, collectivistic individuals look for the loyalty that is associated with
established relationships and put the needs of others first.
Their distinctive characteristics are well defined in Hofstede's
(1980) work in which collectivism signifies a focus on tight or
strong ties, a close-knit bond not only between participants of
nuclear families but also among extended families. The environment in which collectivist people live is most often group
or community based. As a result, according to Hofstede (1997),
collectivistic people "grow up and learn to think of themselves
as part of the 'we' group, a relationship which is not voluntary
but given by nature" (p. 50). For such people, the notion of
group is the accepted and unquestioned way of life.

It is useful to note that collectivistic people make a clear
distinction between in-group and out-group (Tayeb 2003;
Triandis 2002). This distinction is referred to as *we* (in-group)
versus *they* (out-group) and becomes a primary source of
identity and basis for loyalty. This distinction also serves as a
boundary that regulates behavior; it acts as a control mechanism by which individuals determine what, how, why, and to
whom information should or will be disclosed (Petronio 2000).
This boundary effect was evident in our study when collectivistic participants expressed concerns and issues, offered
proposals, or presented their ideas. They seemed to disclose
a great deal of information (i.e., sent lengthy messages) to
the list members because they were considered the in-group,
a cohesive unit formed as they collaborated and worked
together toward common goals. Although we were unable to
compare this behavior with their behavior outside the list environment, the long messages demonstrated that high-context
participants were willing to disclose their ideas in a generously
detailed manner.

The findings also showed that individuals often addressed
other participants explicitly, by name, at the beginning of
their message—very few of them did not mention a name.
Messages sometimes included a formal and polite salutation,

but it was personalized by the use of the recipient's name. This behavior is another sign of relationship orientation. The sending of ambiguous messages with restricted codes also suggests that they viewed other listserv participants as we, since their vagueness indicates that they assumed that the recipient would know exactly what the message was based on or what context was being referred to.

This assumption of common knowledge is typical of high-context communication. As Hall (1976) demonstrated, when high-context people communicate, they often economize on their words because they share the same context, and thus few words are needed. In face-to-face communication, body language, facial expressions, and gestures serve as signals or cues to what the message means. When high-context people communicate in the absence of nonverbal cues, some of the information necessary for interpretation is stripped out, making it difficult to decode the message. In these situations, high-context participants often develop compensatory behaviors (Walther and Parks 2002); this study uncovered several examples such as the use of emoticons to stand in for the tone of voice or expression. Some examples are "sounds pretty good to me! ☺" or "For more efficient use of capacities and 'diversity in real space', ☺ may I suggest that ..."

Task Oriented versus Relationship Oriented

With the task-oriented Civil Society decision-making behaviors, low-context participants demonstrated high levels of concern for task orientation; they focused on pragmatic goals, resulting in decisions that were factually based most of the time. According to Triandis (2002), people who are individualistic place more emphasis on rationality and thus make decisions based on linear thinking or logic, whereas people who are collectivistic place more emphasis on relatedness, making decisions more on emotional or expressive grounds. As he explains it, "rationality

refers to the careful computation of costs and benefits of relationship" while "relatedness refers to giving priority to relationships and taking into account the need of others, even when
such relationships are not advantageous to the individual" (2002,
p. 24).

The findings in our Civil Society study clearly reflect
the above arguments that were made by Triandis, Zakaria,
Stanton, and Sarkar-Barney. For example, Civil Society participants who are individualistic usually sent emails with firm
deadlines and clear instructions, such as when and how to
send documents in order to meet a deadline. These people
were more concerned with the outcome: meeting a deadline.
The tone of the message was highly task oriented, as shown
by the fact that no other subjects were mentioned. For example, messages like "please send the document by [date]..."
were quite common among individualistic participants in the
plenary listserv. The obvious goal of such messages is instrumental, and relationship is a secondary objective (if present at
all).

Based on the above findings, those GVT members who
held individualistic goals clearly reflected their behaviors
through their task-oriented messages, which emphasize *what
to do* and *who will do it*—the structures, procedures, and
guidelines. Task-oriented messages are often straightforward
and short, although they can sometimes be lengthy if they
contain instructions and procedures. The following short message sent by Kathryn highlights the things that needed to be
accomplished:

> Hi Jimmy Punnel,
>   We are working on a French translation—this is
> all voluntary work so if you have any contacts, much
> appreciated...
> Kathryn

Or this similar brief message from Renee:

Dear Adrian,

Sorry and thanks for reminding. Program and registration form can be downloaded from www .ngocongo.org. Click at WSIS.

Renee

On the other hand, a task-oriented message may contain an agenda or the context for a meeting. For example, Edul sent this invitation out:

I'd like to invite you to the first meeting of the Multi-stakeholders Partnerships Familly of the CSB.

The agenda of the meeting will include the family organization, the definition of the mission and pro-gramming of activities. Room A, ITU, September 16, from 2 PM to 4 PM.

Please, send me an email to register (only to know the number of interested people) and help me to invite more organizations by announcing this invita-tion around you.

Edul Zaki

Another example of a task-oriented message is one that provides clear instructions about a deadline to be met. This straightforward message from Kathryn provides relevant infor-mation so the recipients would know exactly what to do.

Dear all

If you would like to comment on the Civil Society Draft Response to the 19th September Declaration, please send comments to: ct@wsis-cs.org (not plenary @wsis-cs.org) by 12 pm today.

Please send **exact text** not general comments as we won't have time to edit/process lengthy comments.

thanks

Kathryn

Many of the messages also illustrated the *relationship-oriented* construct. It was evident from the messages that this construct was an accurate description of the socialization of the participants. The behaviors reflected in the messages showed that the participants attempted to establish some kind of rapport or build networks and associations among and within the Civil Society participants. In the messages, participants refer explicitly to other participants when responding to a message, for example, "Thank you and Timothy Rhodes for all of your hard work at completing the reports and placing them on the Internet." The tone was definitely formal and yet personal. Another example of relationship-oriented behavior was when participants wrote courteous and warm phrases in the very first paragraph. For example, Sandra dedicated one of her messages simply to express gratitude:

> I just want to thank everyone for the comments, expressions of appreciation and constructive criticism that has come in on the priorities document. With more time we could no doubt have polished the text further, but I think we have made important progress in including more concrete proposals in relation to previous documents.
> I also want to thank everyone who has worked hard on getting the document out. This was a truly collective effort and the writing was shared among a large group of people.
> Sandra

Relationship-oriented people do not plunge into the subject matter right away, nor do they state their opinions explicitly in the opening paragraph. They first give a salutation or a greeting, followed by a courtesy statement. Their opinion or purpose only comes in the second paragraph or late in the first paragraph, as exemplified in the following illustration (emphasis added in bold and characteristic features identified in square brackets):

Dear Mr. Kiefer, [formal salutation]
Thank you for your comments [statement of courtesy] on the document presented on behalf of the Civil Society, endorsed, amongst others, by the organization I represent. As you suggest, there is a lot to discuss. That's exactly the idea of the World Summit.

As for your last observation, concerning "something called community media", I would like to mention [statement of opinion] that we are talking about a huge and massive global phenomenon, that prioritizes the use of communication for social objectives. Your insinuations in the direction of state intervention communication ("mouthpieces for central or local authorities") are absolutely incorrect. Community media seek to fortify the democratization of communication by active participation of all actors in society, privileging the normally absent ones (indigenous, women, youth, poor etc.).

Comments were made by our representatives in the Intersessional Meeting in Paris that "the media family" made observations about the document presented by Civil Society. As you are acting as coordinator of this family, and being myself a member of this 'family', representing the Latin American Association of Educational Radio (ALER, with 107 members in Latin America), I would like to remember [statement of tactfulness or diplomacy] you that, as far as I am informed, there wasn't any kind of consultation organized amongst the members of the media family. I duely respect your opinion [statement of tactfulness/diplomacy] as a member of Civil Society, but would ask you to respect the diversity

of opinions within the media family whenever you speak publicly on behalf of it.
Kind Regards,
Verner Vinson
P.D. Could you please be so kind [pleasant closure] to inform us, the members of the Media Family, who else are being part of this important organizational body of the WSIS process?

In the preceding case, Verner clearly expresses his disagreement and disappointment with the lack of respect that was shown to him and his group, but he presents it in a subtle, polite, and indirect manner. The tone of the message is delicate and diplomatic, but one can clearly understand the underlying message. Obviously, the writer is attempting to maintain a harmonious atmosphere for relationship's sake, instead of creating conflict. He also sends the message with a gracious tone by saying "please be so kind..." In short, high-context individuals have more procedures or stages of communicating disagreement or discussing contentious issues.

Another insight from messages such as the following is that people not only care about the tasks to be accomplished or deadline to be met but also the well-being of the other participants. Fostering good relationships was one of their main concerns before discussing other issues. Renee's message is a good example of this; it is affectionate and warm, and this tone obviously indicates the importance that she places on relationships.

Dear all,
I hope you made it all safely home or are otherwise relaxing.
A quick response to questions which came up in the last CT-Group regarding side events during PrepCom-3: The Secretariat told us that no official side events/roundtables are planned, because all time and energy will be fixed on the negotiations.

However, NGOs/CSOs who want to organize a lunch time presentation/panel event can do so, but are responsible for the organization.

CONGO will keep you up date via www.prepcom .net/wsis where you will find also complete coverage of the Intersessional meeting.

I would like to thank CS Bureau, CS-CT, caucuses and all who worked hard to move CS presence forward. Although CS participation is still an uphill struggle, many governments have recognized the value of our contributions.

A big thanks also to the Secretariat, to Louise and her team, for all her support.

Have a nice summer!

Best

Renee

In a similar vein, some participants made many references to others by name, which showed that there were relational bonds among these people. Because many of the messages did not use specific names or refer to any person explicitly, mentioning names suggest that the writer knows and likes/respects that person, either from personal contact (face-to-face meetings) or through their correspondences via the email listserv. For example, Isuzuki explicitly thanks specific individuals in the very first line of his message: "Akihari and all, I appreciate your hard work and good result", or Marta's note to Kathryn: "Hi Kathryn! I was reading your paper…It's very interesting" or Rince's positive response: "MS, Indeed, this is a very good proposal."

As a summary, it is crucial to take into account how people communicate their goals in the decision-making process. The communicative behaviors are dependent on whether they are high- or low-context members. In specific, low-context members who subscribed to individualistic cultural values displayed task-oriented email messages for achieving the planned outcomes and goals. Hence, the messages are straightforward and concise.

High-context members who are from collectivistic cultures prefer to share messages that are highly warm in their tone. However, the messages could also be as objective in their plans and implementation as people from an individualistic culture. In essence, the distinctive approaches and styles of communication lie in the manner that the messages are communicated in different cultures.

References

Adler, N.J. 1997. *International Dimensions of Organizational Behavior*, 3rd ed. Cincinnati, OH: South-Western.

Hall, E.T. 1976. *Beyond Culture*. Garden City, NJ: Anchor Books/Doubleday.

Hofstede, G. 1980. *Culture's Consequences: International Differences in Work-Related Values*. Beverly Hills, CA: SAGE Publications.

Hofstede, G. 1997. *Cultures and Organizations: Software of the Mind*, 1st ed. New York: McGraw-Hill.

Mills, J. and Clark, M.S. 1982. Exchange and communal relationships. In L. Wheeler (Ed.), *Review of Personality and Social Psychology* (pp. 121–144). Beverly Hills, CA: SAGE.

Petronio, S. (Ed.). 2000. *Balancing the Secrets of Private Disclosures*. Mahwah, NJ: LEA Publishers.

Tayeb, M. 2003. *International Management: Theories and Practices*. Essex: Pearson Education Limited.

Triandis, H.C. 2002. Generic individualism and collectivism. In M.J. Gannon & K.L. Newman (Eds.), *The Blackwell Handbook of Cross-Cultural Management* (pp. 16–46). Malden, MA: Blackwell Publisher.

Walther, J.B. & Parks, M.R. 2002. Cues filtered out, cues filtered in: Computer-mediated communication and relationships. In M.L. Knapp & J.A. Daly (Eds.), *Handbook of Interpersonal Communication*, 3rd ed. (pp. 529–563). Thousand Oaks, CA: SAGE.

Zakaria, N., Stanton, J.M. & Sarkar-Barney, S.T.M. 2003. Designing and implementing culturally-sensitive IT applications: The interaction of culture values and privacy issues in the Middle East. *Information Technology & People*, 16, 49–75.

STRATEGIES AND COMPETENCIES FOR MANAGING GLOBAL VIRTUAL TEAMS

V

Working together at a distance.

Marion Cliff was baffled and frustrated with the way that people were working in her virtual teams. After much contemplation, it dawned on her that there were some important differences between working with her teams on-site in Taiwan and her teams in the Texas office. For instance, what about having to wait up late or into the wee hours to have a Skype meeting with your colleagues in another continent when you have already devoted a good 9–10 hours at the office that day? Working with people who miss deadlines regularly because they perceive time as flexible and feel that timelines can be adjusted and stretched based on their schedule? Working with people who keep silent when things go wrong because they feel that they should try to solve it—until it's too late and things can no longer be fixed? Many other things occurred to her that might be equally incomprehensible to her team members. Not only was she working with people who were at a distance, but they were also strangers to begin with. This was very different from working on-site at an office, where you know everyone's strengths, weaknesses, and personal quirks!

Chapter 14

What Global Leaders Should Know about Managing "Working Together at a Distance"

Introduction

Over the past few decades, management theory has encouraged organizations to stride ahead, confident in the belief that leaders can be developed and shaped into a winning character, defying the widespread maxim that "Leaders are born, not made!" However, with the 21st century's impetus of globalization, organizations have transformed the workplace into a boundaryless, innovative, and multicultural structure. This new phenomenon has forced organizations to create strategies that demand global leaders who are competent in managing virtual teams that thrive on diversity in many forms. Appropriate cross-cultural training needs to be developed and disseminated because the current workplace is composed not only of teams that are made up of heterogeneous members but also teams whose members are noncollocated and are strangers to one another. To recruit and retain talents who can shepherd a multicultural team to success in the virtual workplace may seem like a daunting task for a human resource manager. Instead, it may be more useful for a firm to train its own people as global leaders to prepare them for dealing with cross-cultural nuances and benefit from the synergies that are created by heterogeneous team members. In the context of global virtual teams (GVTs), then, the challenge is what strategies should a firm employ to nurture and develop global leaders who are culturally sensitive and competent to build and manage a high-performing GVT? Does it require diverse leadership characteristics, traits, values, and expectations?

Consider the culturally rooted challenges in the global virtual workplace that is illustrated in the scenario mentioned earlier in this section. What are the chances that such a situation could create conflict, frustration, confusion, and misunderstanding between multicultural, noncollocated team members? As a consequence of these difficulties, a company may find itself with demotivated and uncommitted employees. The reality is that, in many typical multinational corporations (MNCs), working at a distance is challenging and stressful, yet it can also be rewarding and exciting if handled properly. For instance, people no longer need to travel thousands of miles or suffer the turmoil and uncertainty of relocation and adjustment, while the company avoids the cost of cross-cultural counseling to prepare them for the expatriation process and the cultural shocks that they might encounter. The noncollocated workspace offers an innovative work structure in which many operating costs can be reduced or even eliminated. Similarly, many employees may find such opportunities deeply satisfying, since they can learn from and about diverse multicultural management and leadership styles.

On the other hand, cultural diversity poses heightened difficulties, and it can be a real challenge for people who have never had the opportunity to work in a GVT structure. Even those who have had GVT experience may still find it difficult to accomplish their goals due to inexperience in managing both the cultural and virtual aspects of this work structure. In each new heterogeneous team, leaders need to find unique ways to manage members and allow new ways of working to emerge out of different cultural values, attitudes, and practices. At the organizational level, the key questions for the human resource manager include the following: How can we recruit new talent and new executives who can fit into the GVT structure? How can we train and develop culturally competent global leaders who are able to deal with virtual teams that are composed of diverse cultural backgrounds? Does an employee have what it takes to work in a virtual work structure? How many will be willing to put up with these new challenges when their workload or responsibilities in their own office are competitive and demanding? With such questions in mind, how does the human resource manager strategically plan for their human capital? For example, should candidates be told in detail about the GVT structure during their interview, or should they be allowed to independently learn about it over time?

In previous studies, scholars in the field of international human resource management have clearly established that failures in expatriate international assignments may be due to many factors: inability to adjust to the environment, the lack of tolerance from spouse and children, homesickness, inadequate cultural orientation and preparation from their organization, mismatched levels of expectations regarding achievement and goals, uncompetitive and insufficient compensation and financial packages, and many others (Harzing 1995; Mendenhall & Wiley 1994; Bird & Dunbar 1991; Oddou 1991; Tung 1987).

Nowadays, the work landscape has changed because multinational organizations depend heavily on GVTs to exploit the synergistic values of human capital and eclectic talents working at a distance. The physical workplace has become a virtual workspace offering high mobility, flexibility, and accessibility. As the saying goes, "Two heads are better than one" (or "Alone, we can do so little; together, we can do so much"); this suggests the potential benefits if organizations fully commit to the use of such teams. On the other hand, the lack of opportunity to meet in person may pose psychological, managerial, and behavioral challenges. Despite this drawback, one of the key advantages of GVTs is that firms do not need to send their executives to a foreign country, and thus people no longer need to relocate. Firms can save the cost of expatriation; managers can avoid the stress of culture shock frequently experienced by expatriates; and international human resource managers no longer need to help expatriate employees cope with the multiple issues that come with living in an unfamiliar country.

Yet I question whether the GVT structure can totally eliminate the impact of culture shock, since these teams will include people from different cultures. GVTs are largely dependent on or composed of heterogeneous members. Does this imply that GVT members will experience *virtual cultural shock?* After all, culture shock can arise from various sources: working with strangers with whom one has no shared historical background and who have diverse communication styles, different uses and functional roles of technology, large time differences, and many others. Obviously, GVT members do not need to undergo the expatriation process and its associated stresses: no relocating agenda, no fuss of travelling for long hours on the plane, no issues of family adjustment, no orientation to a new workplace, no repatriation difficulties when they return home, and so on. But the cultural nuances remain. GVT members will experience culture shock but in a different manner; they will still need to adjust to their colleagues' cultural nuances and learn to work with strangers in a virtual work sphere.

The findings of my research on GVTs and the use of email have several important implications for the leaders of multinational and international organizations, particularly with respect to cross-cultural collaboration in a distributed environment.

The collapse of the traditional hierarchical structure and the emergence of a more flexible, loose organizational structure provide new opportunities for collaboration by reducing the barriers of geographical distance and time zones. Specifically, my work offers an increased transparency and a greater understanding of the diverse management styles and multiplicity of cultures facing MNCs, and suggests methods for building a more effective cross-cultural training that will boost cultural awareness and sensitivity, teaching appropriate behaviors for overcoming cultural differences, developing intercultural online communication competencies, and designing culturally sensitive information technology applications for effective electronic collaborative and communication tools. All of these practical elements serve the goal of enabling people to collaborate effectively at a distance using a sociotechnical infrastructure that is compatible and congruent with their varying cultural value orientations and ideologies.

Leaders in MNCs who will manage GVTs need to consider several elements that are central to any discussions of culture and GVTs. These elements are based on the following perspectives.

Cultural Adjustments

Executives sent on assignment to a foreign country by their parent company are known as expatriates. An expatriate is a person who lives and works in a foreign country, relocating from his or her home country to a host country. Expatriates will generally work in the host country for a certain number of years and need to adjust accordingly. Such adjustment is known as the *expatriation process*, whereby people learn to behave in accordance with the host country's norms based on their observations of others. According to the classic model introduced by Oberg (1960), the expatriation process has four phases. The first is the *honeymoon* phase in which executives

or managers experience a sense of euphoria when management asks them to move to another country. Everything seems
encouraging and delightful. They are excited, anticipating that
they will get global exposure, gain knowledge and expertise,
and perhaps get promoted. During the honeymoon phase,
expatriates view travel to a new and exciting foreign land as
an excellent opportunity. They look forward to a new workplace with challenging tasks and new people with new behaviors, values, and attitudes. At this stage, people usually do not
regret the decision to go far away from home. They feel fully
prepared to take on the challenges, and, when they arrive at
their new workplace, they encounter warm greetings from
their new colleagues, a pleasant boss, and a friendly work
environment conducive to success.

In Oberg's second stage, conflicts begin to arise due to
culture shock, which is the inability to adjust and assimilate to the new culture in the host country. According to
Browaeys and Price (2010), the concept of culture shock
was introduced as far back as the late 1950s. Culture shock
is defined as the uncertainty and anxiety that arise when
people are confronted with a new culture and subsequently
experience feelings of loss, confusion, and social and
cultural unimportance/low status in the new workplace.
Culture shock also occurs when an executive encounters
conflicts that are rooted in clashing cultural values, norms,
and rituals. As one might expect, culture shock usually leads
to unpleasant consequences. Numerous studies have established that many expatriates fail in their international assignments (Bird & Dunbar 1991; Oddou 1991). Instead of staying
abroad for the committed number of years, they came back
much earlier than expected, sometimes within less than a
year. What happened? What are the causes? If an expatriate fails to tolerate and accept the difficulties encountered
in his or her new locale, both the home country and the
host country management will be disappointed, their colleagues will be left with many perplexing questions, and

their families will be apprehensive and disheartened. What is the cause of this expatriation disappointment? Is it due to the difficulty of accepting culturally related changes during this stage?

The third phase in the expatriation process is adjustment or stability. To reach this phase, the expatriate must fully understand the nature and characteristics of the host culture and accept the cultural differences. One of the defining characteristics of culture is that it is learned by a society or group of people over time rather than inherited. Culture is also dynamic (not static) and transferable from one generation to another. Therefore, from a cultural standpoint, the adjustment process, as experienced by an expatriate, can have different outcomes. According to Rice & Rogers (1980), people first go through the process of screening cultural characteristics and selecting which to adopt. People evaluate these new cultural characteristics based on whether they are (1) better or more useful, (2) consistent with existing practices, (3) easily learned, (4) identifiable through trial and error, and (5) recognized as beneficial by all people ascribing to that society. Second, this cultural borrowing is a reciprocal process. People who undergo the organizational and cultural change and the people who are making the changes need to be equally accepting. It cannot be a one-way process. Third, the transference of culture may not be flawless; that is, newcomers to the culture may not recreate or adopt it in its original form; they may eliminate some things and introduce new things. Leaders may model certain practices by making modifications to fit with the current context and culture, both organizational and national. Fourth, it is not easy to transfer the patterns of behaviors, belief systems, and values (p. 179, para 2). As Ferraro (2010) says, "[S]ome cultural practices are more easily diffused than others" (p. 33). There is a strong interaction between organizational culture and the indigenous or local culture. In order to understand the organizational leadership of an organization, we need to observe both the impact of organizational culture on leadership practices and the influence of national cultural values on the development of leadership behaviors.

The last phase is called adaptation. In this stage, expatriates have attuned their minds, emotions, and behaviors to a new way of doing things. Simply awareness and acceptance are insufficient; expatriates must be able to assimilate and acculturate to the new way of doing things in their host country. Some people adopt a certain value because it is similar to their own or because it lets them exercise both their lifestyle and work values. What makes people resist accepting new values? Some of the cultural values observed in the new workplace may not be consistent with their own. Other cultural values take time to change—for example, time orientation. In some cultures, people think nothing of coming to a meeting 15 minutes late; this lateness is part and parcel of the way that they do things at work since, for them, time is not money and is therefore relatively unimportant. This may be difficult to accept for someone from a culture that values time and punctuality and considers it wasteful not to meet due dates and deadlines. Similarly, in a high power distance culture, the boss will walk into a meeting and tell everyone what needs to be done, giving instructions without further discussions. Their authority is a manifestation of the bureaucratic and hierarchical organizational structures within which they function and is a symbol of status, but it may be off-putting to someone who is accustomed to a more collegial boss/employee relationship. All these cultural values embedded in one's thinking, perceptions, and actions take time to change. People cannot change overnight, even if the organization has trained them in and exposed them to diverse cultural values. Changes in human behavior are hard to achieve because internal change takes longer than changes to systems, infrastructures, and policy. Yet acculturation must take place for expatriates to achieve a smooth adaptation.

Are You Experiencing Virtual Cultural Shock?

For many decades, knowledge of the expatriation process has allowed organizations to plan for the impact of expatriate employees' adjustments when they first move to a host country. A new workplace means a high probability of adjustment failure, dependent on the cultural distance between the home and the host country and the degree of shift from the old to the new value orientation. Despite the reduction in culture shock when a person no longer has to travel thousands of miles, a new process of adjustment takes place reflecting the impact of cultural shocks on the virtual work structure. In the GVT context, global leaders still need to manage a similar cultural adjustment process because team members come from many different cultural backgrounds. Global leaders need to understand the team process: how it is formed and how it functions. Tuckman and Jensen's (1977) teamwork model illustrates the typical process of team development (refer to Figure 14.1).

According to Tuckman and Jensen, in the first phase, *forming*, members begin the process of getting to know each other. This is an *ice-breaker* stage wherein members are strangers to one another; they have little or no understanding of the

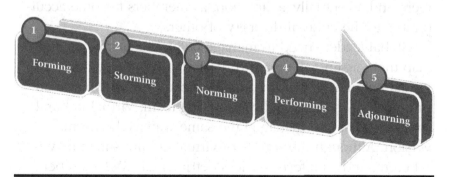

Figure 14.1   Stages of group development. (From Tuckman, B.W. & Jensen, M.C., *Group and Organizational Studies*, 2, 419–427, 1977.)

other team members or of their past performance. At this point, people will be in the honeymoon phase; they will be excited and enthusiastic about meeting their GVT colleagues for the first time and looking forward to starting the project, although they have no grounds as yet to trust one another. In the second stage, *storming*, members may experience conflicts or difficulties in adjusting to their tasks. This stage is where culture shock often occurs. During this stage, the team members undergo a negotiation process in which roles, deadlines, responsibilities, and tasks are spelled out, and a leader is assigned or emerges; this process allows them to begin to understand and trust one another. At this stage, continued conflict or a mishandled crisis can damage this trust that is beginning to develop.

During the next stage, known as *norming*, team members develop a clearer understanding of what needs to be done; norms, procedures, and routines are put in place; and conflicts are resolved. The stage is also known as adjustment because, by this time, team members have learned a little about each other and have begun to trust one another despite their cultural nuances and differences. During the next stage, *performing*, teams become more comfortable with one another; at this stage, trust is fully developed, and people work as cohesively as possible. This stage also prepares team members for adjustment and, eventually, adaptation, as members become acculturated to the cultural diversity of others.

Global leaders need to manage cultural adjustments and map them against the teamwork model to understand how virtual cultural shock can be minimized or even eliminated in order to achieve a high-performing team. Virtual cultural shock needs to be managed the same way as the normal version. Although the source of virtual culture shock may be different, and its effects are less detrimental, GVT members will still encounter such challenges because the *stranger* phenomenon is at work. A stranger can be conceptualized when team members are assembled to work on a project without the opportunities to meet each other either before or after the project takes off. It is a common strategy for many MNCs to cut the cost of travelling and expatriation, and thus, oftentimes, members do engage, communicate, and collaborate without meeting with each other face to face and have to learn to develop trust over time. It is only when the initial crisis of adjustment to one another has been resolved that norms are established, team members perform optimally as trust strengthens, the dynamics of the team evolve, and collaboration becomes more solid. The successful accomplishment of intermediate goals will further reinforce the trust that is being built. In the last stage, *adjourning*, their tasks have been accomplished, and the team members disperse, perhaps experiencing a feeling of loss since they have developed relationships and friendships with their colleagues.

Trust formation varies across the five stages; global leaders need to understand the level of trust and the speed (or slowness) of its growth in each of the stages. Each stage will have different challenges that need to be managed appropriately and in congruence with the cultural preferences and styles of the team's members.

References

Bird, A. & Dunbar, R. 1991. Getting the job done over there: Improving expatriate productivity. *National Productivity Review*, 10(2), 145–156.

Browaeys, M.-J. & Price, R. 2010. *Understanding Cross Cultural Management*. London: Prentice Hall.

Ferraro, G.P. 2010. *The Cultural Dimension of International Business*. Upper Saddle River, NJ: Prentice Hall.

Harzing, A.W. 1995. The persistent myth of high expatriate failure rates. *International Journal of Human Resource Management*, 6, 457–475.

Mendenhall, M.E. & Wiley, C. 1994. Strangers in a strange land: The relationship between expatriate adjustment and impression management. *American Behavioral Scientist*, 37(5), 605–620.

Oberg, K. 1960. Cultural shock: Adjustment to new cultural environments. *Practical Anthropology*, 7, 177–182.

Oddou, G. 1991. Managing your expatriates: What the successful firms do. *Human Resource Planning*, 14(4), 301–309.

Rice, R.E. & Rogers, E.M. 1980. Reinvention in the innovation process. *Knowledge Creation, Diffusion and Utilization*, 1(4), 499–514.

Tuckman, B.W. & Jensen, M.C. 1977. Stages of small group development revisited. *Group and Organizational Studies*, 2, 419–427.

Tung, R.L. 1987. Expatriate assignments: Enhancing success and minimising failure. *Academy of Management Executive*, 1(2), 117–126.

Chapter 15

Why GVT Leaders Need Intercultural Competencies

Intercultural Competency Is Indispensable to Global Virtual Teams

Why does culture matter in a teamwork environment? Specifically, in what ways does culture matter when teams are collaborating in a virtual space—when they are *working together at a distance?* Hall (1976) asserted that "culture is communication and communication is culture" (p. 65). A person's culture and communication cannot be separated, since both are intertwined and interdependent in terms of attitudes, values, and behaviors. The research that I have conducted clearly demonstrates that cultural behaviors are derived from the communication style and that the communication style is rooted in cultural values.

Challenges arise when teams use computer-mediated technology for communicating because such platforms lack the nonverbal cues that are essential for cultures that depend on context for effective communication. Other cultures depend largely on text, whether written or verbal; for them, using computer-mediated technology as a platform for collaboration makes cultural differences less salient, thus equalizing the team members' ability to work together. Inevitably, a wide range of challenges can arise that intensify the effects of culture on global virtual teams (GVTs); such issues need to be directly and openly addressed, hence the need for global leaders to have strong cultural competencies. Past studies have clearly established the contradictory effects of culture on the GVT performance. Whereas some scholars agree that culture does influence the way people manage and collaborate in a team setting (Cogburn & Levinson 2003), others argue that culture has no impact on the way that people collaborate when using computer-mediated communication (CMC) (Shachaf 2008).

The readiness of an organization to fully employ the GVT work structure is directly dependent on developing GVT leaders and team members who are culturally competent. In this chapter, I present what I call the cognition, emotion, and behaviors (CAB) of intercultural competency. These three aspects form the answers to crucial questions such as "Are you aware of and knowledgeable about different cultural values? Can you tolerate and be sensitive to the cultural nuances of others? Can you emulate and then acculturate to new cultural values and reshape your behaviors accordingly?" First, however, let us define the concept of intercultural competency.

What Is Intercultural Competency?

Ferraro (2010) defines culture as "everything that people have, think and do as members of their society" (p. 20). In the "Cultural Characteristics" section in Chapter 4, I use the *onion model* (Barsoux & Schneider 1998) to illustrate the many layers of culture: artifacts, values/beliefs, and basic assumptions and behaviors. GVT leaders need to be familiar with Ferraro's definition, as well as the idea of multiple layers of culture, in order to competently manage team members with different cultural backgrounds. Koester et al. (1993) conceptualized intercultural competence as having three aspects: (1) culture-general understanding, (2) culture-specific understanding, and (3) positive regard of the other. Chen and Starosta (1997) suggested that the *process* of developing intercultural communication competence also has three aspects: (1) cultural awareness, (2) cultural sensitivity, and (3) cultural adroitness. These findings suggest that leaders need to observe what people think and do by practicing awareness, sensitivity, and specific behavioral approaches. One way of thinking about this is the CAB Intercultural Competency Framework, discussed in depth as follows.

Acculturation is the process whereby people learn to behave in a particular way based on their observations of a cultural role model. In the context of GVTs, team members need to fully understand the cultural differences present within the team before acculturation can take place. Each member of the team needs to acknowledge and recognize how he or she works within the team environment, as well as how and why others work the way that they do. Team members must not only tolerate but also accept these differences if their heterogeneous team is to be successful. An important role of the GVT leader is to model proper behavior for their team and help their team members become aware of their behavioral characteristics. Acculturation is not merely about changing one's personality or character; rather, it means each person adapting to and shaping the way that the team works so that the team can blend together into a smoothly functioning unit. The GVT work structure also demands changes in the way that people communicate and collaborate since it requires the use of CMC, including social media tools such as Facetime, Skype, WhatsApp, Twitter, Messenger, and so on.

Some might question the need for culturally competent GVT leaders when the team members may never meet in person, since they are collaborating at a distance. In fact,

GVT leaders will confront many cultural idiosyncrasies, even—sometimes, especially—in the virtual workplace. For example, team members will likely bring to the table different management practices, communication styles, decision-making and negotiation styles, conflict resolution methods, and time management ideas, among other things. Skilled GVT leaders will be able to find the right fit and balance between their own cultural values and the new multicultural context in which they are now operating. Additionally, leaders will need to encourage cultural awareness within the team using the knowledge and information that they acquired during cross-cultural training and instill cultural sensitivity by fostering tolerance and appreciation and by modeling the desired behaviors. In other words, they need to take action in the right way.

To build high-performing GVTs, organizations must develop cross-cultural competencies in their employees. These cultural competencies need to align with and accommodate the GVT work structure. To be effective leaders, as well as managers, employees will need to develop strong cultural competencies, incorporating a high level of cultural awareness, sensitivity, and behavior. With respect to GVTs, team members need to develop a similar set of skills as expatriates who travel, work, and live in another country. Unlike expatriate employees, GVT members need not adjust to *living* abroad, but, in a sense, they are still *working* abroad, and, as such, they will undergo the same cognitive and emotional challenges of adjusting to people of different cultures. The process is similar to the expatriation adjustment process, though without all its phases. For example, working with new colleagues who are total strangers may require a high degree of awareness of how others think and function. People need to be culturally savvy when working with others who have different work styles, time management habits, decision-making processes, negotiation skills, and so on. These differences may be detrimental to team success if they are not properly understood and appreciated.

CAB Intercultural Competency Framework

Cultural competency has three aspects, which, together, form the basis for the CAB Intercultural Competency Framework (Zakaria 2000; Chen & Starosta 1997):

1. *Cognitive*—cultural awareness—*what* is culture, and *who* is affected by it? At this level, people form perceptions about others who are different from themselves. They begin to form perspectives about others, with or without any background knowledge about the specific culture. This aspect, if not modified by the other two, can lead people to formulate stereotypes, defined as a generalized opinion about all the members of a cultural group based on limited knowledge. GVT members will need both general and culture-specific training on what to do and what not to do so as to form accurate, well-rounded perceptions.

2. *Affective*—cultural sensitivity—*why* do we need to understand people who are different from us? At this level, team members may feel threatened or uncomfortable when their way of working is questioned by others. Those who are ignorant of these differences, and of the stress created by them, may unintentionally offend or hurt others.

3. *Behavioral*—cultural adroitness—*how* can we better understand other people's differences? *What* actions can we take that are appropriate and relevant to the people whom we are leading and managing? *When* ought we to behave in accordance with a cultural condition or situation? This can be challenging for people with no experience working in an environment where different cultural values come into contact. Team leaders without such experience may not know what to do or how to behave respectfully toward other cultures.

Figure 15.1 demonstrates how these three aspects feed into one another and can be used as a basis for developing all

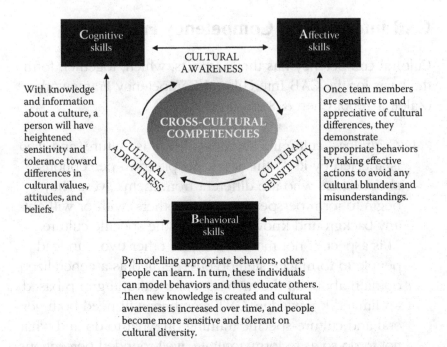

Figure 15.1 CAB Intercultural Competency Framework. (Adapted from Zakaria, N., The possibility of water-cooler chat? Developing communities of practice for knowledge sharing within global virtual teams, in M. Raisinghani (Ed.), *Handbook of Global Information Technology*, Chapter IV (pp. 1–14), New York: Information Science Reference, 2008; Chen, G.M. & Starosta, W.J., *Human Communication*, 1, 1–16, 1997.)

three types of cross-cultural competencies: behavioral, cognitive, and affective (Zakaria 2008).

Some people find working with colleagues from different cultures appealing and exciting, whereas others find it frustrating and challenging. The key questions are whether or not such experiences help to develop and build cultural competency, whether or not they enable participants to discover more about themselves and their own culture, and whether or not it helps participants to know others better.

For example, some people may express frustration with working across time zones since it makes it difficult to interact in real time. Team members in Asia, for example, will be 12 hours apart from their colleagues in North America. Members from the same time zone may end up discussing team business among themselves, leaving their colleagues from other time zones to catch up when they awake. Or ideas may be deliberated at different times, making it difficult to reconcile and negotiate in real time, unless members are willing to split the difference (some stay up late; others get up early) or delay the decision-making process. Many people report that waiting up for meetings off their accustomed time schedule makes them exhausted and anxious. Others report feeling demotivated when their colleagues are not collaborating. Team members may fail to communicate these concerns and simply keep their silence. With such a wide range of cultural challenges, it is important for all team members to be aware of the nuances of cultural values that affect the development of the trust that is necessary for achieving a cohesive team. Some team members will develop a high level of trust for their colleagues based on demonstrated progress toward the set goals—for example, if they see their colleagues working hard to meet deadlines. This approach is known as task orientation. Others will trust their colleagues only after developing a relationship with them—for them, trust evolves naturally over time. This approach is known as relationship orientation. Given these cultural differences, GVT leaders need to carefully manage and harmonize the first stages of forming the team. How can the GVT leader develop a balanced strategy? For example, he or she needs to create a warm and welcoming climate for a group of strangers who are coming into contact with one another for the first time. Some kind of *ice-breaker* activity may speed up the rapport-building stage for those who are relationship oriented. At the same time, for those who are task oriented, the leader will need to incorporate the agenda and goals of the project so that these team members feel a sense of direction and clearly understand the goals.

Organizations, for decades, have spent time planning and organizing various kinds of training for their executives who will be going abroad for international assignments. The same type of training is necessary for those who are virtually going abroad through a GVT. The aim of all these cross-cultural training sessions is to increase the cultural competency of GVT leaders and members who will be working with people from different cultures—an experience similar to that of expatriates. The following subsections explore the three parts of the CAB model in detail.

Cognitive Aspect

Understanding cultural differences usually takes place at the cognitive or thinking level. Cultural competence begins with knowledge about cultural diversity. Cultural values are normally learned first at the cognitive level—whether learning about *other* cultural values or about one's *own* cultural values. At this initial stage, information about unfamiliar culture(s) needs to be first acquired and then fully understood; this may include differences surrounding the basics such as food, climate, language, geography, time, and so on. This cognitive process relies on increasing self-awareness: a good understanding of one's own cultural peculiarities. With this improved understanding, a person can learn to better appreciate others' differences, as well as accurately predict the effects of their behavior on others.

Additionally, at the cognitive level, a person needs to have relevant information and an understanding of culture. Only with the appropriate cultural training, the cultural knowledge can be fully acquired. At this level, once a person obtained concrete knowledge, it allows one to accurately interpret and make sense of the cultural situation that is faced by them. Also, with cultural knowledge, a person will use their intellectual capability to analyze and reason out the cultural challenges faced. Solid cognitive intellectual capacity of cultural differences will lead to cultural sensitivity.

Thus, awareness of oneself and one's own culture is as important as awareness of another's. At the cognitive level, people are expected to know two things: (1) themselves and (2) others. Yet it is difficult for a person to learn about *others* if he or she does not fully know why he himself or she herself does things the way that he or she does. The phrase *knowing me, knowing you* summarizes a balanced approach in which people discover their own and others' cultural values, attitudes, and beliefs. It is human nature not to question one's own culturally learned behaviors—but, when one observes people from another culture and compares what they do with what one normally does, it opens one's eyes. Therefore, a leader needs to learn about the most basic layer of culture by searching for information and building a knowledge base about the new culture(s) that he or she encounters. At this level, both the organization and the leader are responsible for obtaining as much general and specific cultural knowledge as possible.

To have the best hope of success, an organization must provide cross-cultural training for its employees who will be leading GVTs, with the goal of helping managers effectively integrate their GVT members into a cohesive whole. Leaders need to think creatively about how to balance their team's diversity of cultural backgrounds. This is less challenging, obviously, for a leader whose team members all originate from a single country or from culturally similar countries. For example, suppose that a leader from Thailand is asked to manage a team that includes members from South Korea. The leader needs to understand a single new set of cultural values (South Korean). But suppose that a leader from America is asked to manage a GVT that is composed of members from Spain, Japan, and India. This leader now needs to be equipped with an understanding of *three* new cultures. This is the scenario that MNCs often face. The most important skill to develop at this stage is a high level of cultural awareness, built on a thorough knowledge of the culture(s) in question and a mind-set that is attuned to diverse cultural values. Such leaders need to be open minded and mentally prepared so that they can avoid the stereotypical perceptions of members from other cultures.

Affective Aspect

At the second level of cultural competence, a person will
develop emotional intelligence that is useful for understanding culture, and it involves affective skills. A person is
required to look deeper than simple cognitive knowledge or
logic. Once we accept someone's cultural differences at the
rational and cognitive level, we can be tolerant and appreciative of their uniqueness. With concrete cultural knowledge,
at the affective level, a person is expected to develop a high
level of sensitivity when confronted with cultural frustrations.
Once a person is considerate and appreciative of cultural
differences, they will also become composed, patient, and
flexible when faced with myriad cultural complexities. It also
becomes easier for a leader to acknowledge that he or she
is different and to ensure that such differences will not be a
barrier to working together. A person will try to adjust and
take preventive measures to overcome the differences. At this
level also, a person will use their own intuition, wisdom, and
values to make sense of cultural synergies that are obtained
by working with others. In a similar vein, with a strong cognitive foundation, global leaders would become fully aware
of cultural differences, which, in turn, can make them sensitive to cultural nuances.

What is cultural sensitivity? Cultural sensitivity is when a
person is able to put himself or herself in another's shoes, to
accept the differences with an open heart and without emotional strain. Cultural sensitivity is difficult to achieve because
human beings often become emotional when faced with a
situation that they cannot comprehend. Instead of reasoning
things out cognitively, based on logic or knowledge, people
tend to resort to emotions. To overcome this, people must
learn to make inferences and interpret various types of communication. For example, people need to be familiar with both
verbal and nonverbal communication patterns so that they
can communicate equally well with both people who depend

heavily on words and people who rely on cues such as facial expression, body movements, gestures, personal space, and so on. They can then be more sensitive to the body language of others.

To take another example, a person may be aware that, in Asian countries like Malaysia or Indonesia, people generally have a relaxed attitude toward time and are therefore not always punctual. To an outsider, this may come across as a lack of urgency or poor time management. Deadlines may need to be extended. According to Trompenaars and Hampden-Turner (1997), a culture that ascribes to a monochronic time dimension, as do many Western countries (e.g., the United States, Germany), will adhere to time strictly. Time is viewed as linear in which only one thing takes place at a time. On the other hand, for people belonging to a polychronic culture (e.g., Thailand, Indonesia), *time* is flexible, and people can do many things at once. Imagine a GVT leader who needs his or her team to make an important decision; now, imagine that the team is composed of members from both monochronic and polychronic cultures. How might a leader with such knowledge accommodate such differences when he or she needs every team member to make decisions on time and punctually? The leader will need to educate his or her team about such differences so that they can appreciate the timeline of the work and acknowledge an appropriate sensitivity to time. As stated earlier in this section, cultural sensitivity means the ability to perceive and adapt to different situations in order to achieve harmony and cohesiveness among colleagues from diverse cultures.

Behavioral Aspect

By being culturally sensitive, a person will be more observant and perceptive of one's own actions and others' actions. A person will naturally adapt and mimic the behaviors of others to obtain culturally appropriate behaviors. Hence, appropriate

behavior occurs when people have sufficient basic and specific knowledge about a culture and have learned to be tolerant, responsive, and open to cultural differences. Only then
can he or she demonstrate acquired behavioral skills. Armed
with both knowledge and sensitivity, people will perform
more effectively and efficiently in the workplace and interact
cohesively in a GVT.

However, it is not easy to correctly emulate a cultural
behavior without a solid understanding of and sensitivity to
that culture. Human behaviors are complex, even more so
when rooted in different cultural values. Culture is also complex, and this combination of complexities makes it exceed-
ingly difficult for change to happen at the behavioral level.
Human behaviors cannot be changed overnight. It takes time
to change attitudes, perceptions, and values. Only when a
leader keeps an open mind to see and acknowledge the differences within his or her team and an open heart to readily
accept and appreciate those differences can the appropriate
behaviors be modeled and, ideally, emulated. At this stage,
a person may achieve acculturation, wherein he or she has
learned to accept, adapt, and then replicate what is observed.
This process is easier when the person is convinced that there
is a good reason for doing so and is the last stage of achieving cultural competency. A person can also become innovative
through re-creation by performing an action that is based on
his or her understanding and knowledge of culture. Once the
innovative actions and behaviors are acceptable to others in a
particular culture, that new knowledge is further added to the
cognitive intellect of a person.

In the GVT context, people often work with strangers in
a virtual space and cannot observe their physical behaviors.
For such behaviors to be solid, a leader needs to model the
desired behavior for his or her team members. For example,
a communication style that is direct and straightforward can
be perceived as rude and harsh by a culture that appreciates

subtlety and indirection. How can a GVT leader steer deliberation, the discussion of issues, and decision making if he or she
is not sensitive to the various ways that people communicate?
How can a GVT leader avoid cultural blunders that might
harm the group relationship or negatively affect the task to be
accomplished? Leaders need to take a proactive role in modeling the right behaviors for their team. Once the leader shows
the correct way to behave in a culturally fraught situation, the
members can follow suit; this, in turn, promotes a sense of
bonding among the members because they can then work in a
more cohesive manner. Through the right conduct and actions,
members will gain cultural experience and can subsequently
educate others on what is appropriate and inappropriate.
Creation of new knowledge will increase as more people gain
experience working in GVTs.

A leader might have a so-called cultural blind spot, meaning they do not know what a given culture considers required,
acceptable, or taboo. A cultural blind spot could indicate simple ignorance, or it may imply that the person fails to take into
account anything other than what he or she personally finds
acceptable. Such a person is referred to as *ethnocentric*, meaning they hold the belief that their way of doing things is the
best way. GVT leaders need to model culturally appropriate
behaviors by acting in ways that are appropriate and relevant
to the team that they are managing.

In sum, these three aspects are presented as a set of
guidelines for GVT leaders to use in developing their cultural
competency (see Chapter 17). The model is not only based
on sequential stages; it also introduces a cyclical process
wherein any of the stages can take place first and be followed by any of the others. Cultural knowledge is required
before the affective/emotional aspect can be reached, and it
presents the third stage (behavior) as result[ing] when people
have sufficient basic and specific knowledge about a culture
and have learned to be tolerant, responsive, and open to

cultural differences. As the name *CAB* denotes, these represent the basic ingredients for a skillful leader of GVTs. It is useful to note that cultural challenges can arise at any of the stages, and different competencies may be required. An affective issue may arise when a leader reacts emotionally to a cultural disparity; with the right knowledge, however, the leader can suppress his or her instinctive reaction and instead respond with more sensitivity. The cognitive stage may be a trigger point for someone who is ignorant of cultural differences, but, when equipped with the appropriate knowledge, the person may be more appreciative of what he or she perceived at first as silly or ridiculous. The behavioral stage can be puzzling or irritating when a leader observes certain behaviors. As such, the stage can also be an initiating process when a leader observes certain behaviors that are not *the norm*—but, if the leader has the requisite cultural knowledge, he or she can recognize the roots of the behavior and resolve the issue.

In addition to the CAB intercultural framework, there are many other dimensions on which leaders can build competency. For instance, Adrian Furnham (http://adrianfurnham .com), a renowned behavioral psychologist and professor with experience in teaching more than 28 nationalities in the United Kingdom, points out that "The world is getting smaller each day and although we may be ethnically different, human beings are quite homogenous" (*Friday Magazine*). He argues that leaders can be trained and developed and that there is not necessarily such a thing as a *born leader*. Cultural differences need not be a barrier to becoming a competent global leader, since any individual with sufficient inspiration and dedication can choose to educate himself or herself culturally. Furnham identifies seven dimensions that organizations can use when developing cross-culturally competent leaders (see Table 15.1).

Table 15.1   Dimensions of Global Leadership in the Context of GVTs

Leadership Dimension	Cultural Context
Cultural immersion	Ability to acculturate to a new environment with different cultural values, beliefs, and behaviors
Capability	Possession of the necessary leadership skills, both in qualifications and experience
Care	Ability to be compassionate, to express empathy for and care about the well-being of those whom they lead
Connection	Ability to interact effectively with a variety of people, develop relationships, and make connections easily
Consciousness	Awareness of one's surroundings and of the changes in one's environment, particularly when dealing with cultural diversity
Context	Possession of a well-defined perspective for developing measures and strategies to cope with a GVT's cultural dynamics
Contrast	Ability to compare cultural behaviors

References

Barsoux, J.-L. & Schneider, S.C. 1997. *Managing Across Cultures.* London: Prentice Hall.

Chen, G.M. & Starosta, W.J. 1997. A review of the concept of intercultural sensitivity. *Human Communication*, 1, 1–16.

Cogburn, D.L. & Levinson, N.S. 2003. US-Africa virtual collaboration in globalization studies: Success factors for complex, cross-national learning teams. *International Studies Perspectives*, 4, 34–51.

Ferraro, G.P. 2010. *The Cultural Dimension of International Business*. Upper Saddle River, NJ: Prentice Hall.

Hall, E.T. 1976. *Beyond Culture*. Garden City, NJ: Anchor Books/ Doubleday.

Koester, J., Wiseman, R.L. & Sanders, J.A. 1993. Multiple perspectives of intercultural communication competence. In R.L. Wiseman & J. Koester (Eds.), *Intercultural Communication Competence [International and Intercultural Communication Annual]*, 17 (pp. 3–15). Newbury Park, CA: SAGE.

Shachaf, P. 2008. Cultural diversity and information and communication technology impacts on global virtual teams: An exploratory study. *Information and Management*, 45(2), 131–142.

Trompenaars, F. & Hampden-Turner, C. 1997. *Riding the Waves of Culture: Understanding Diversity in Global Business*. New York: McGraw-Hill.

Zakaria, N. 2000. The effects of cross-cultural training on the acculturation process of the global workforce. *International Journal of Manpower*, 21(6), 492–510.

Zakaria, N. 2008. The possibility of water-cooler chat? Developing communities of practice for knowledge sharing within global virtual teams. In M. Raisinghani (Ed.), *Handbook of Global Information Technology*, Chapter IV (pp. 1–14). New York: Information Science Reference.

Chapter 16

How to Manage GVTs—Dos and Don'ts for Culture and Decision Making for Global Leaders

Introduction

In a multinational corporate setting, a global virtual team (GVT) leader must be culturally competent so that he or she can maximize the synergistic value of working in a heterogeneous team. In addition, a GVT leader must be technologically competent in order to fully exploit the multifunctional collaborative tools necessary for working virtually. In this chapter, I provide some useful decision-making strategies for GVT managers that take into account the influence of differing cultures. I provide culturally based guidelines in terms of the *dos and don'ts* for managing GVTs effectively and developing high-performing teams.

A key question that arises that global leaders in multinational corporations need to deal with when managing GVTs is "How do cultural values influence the decision-making process?" Hence, in this chapter, we look at one example: a study of the contributions of the globally distributed members of the World Summit on the Information Society (WSIS) Civil Society to the decision-making process. Based on a broad analysis of their *overall* participation in the decision-making process, the study's findings showed significant differences between members with high-context (HC) and low-context (LC) communicative orientations. Culture, in the form of intercultural communication styles and cultural values, does indeed have an impact on the manner in which members participate in the decision-making process and the strategies that they employ (Adler 1997). This was visible in the behaviors of Civil Society participants at all stages, from the initial expression of their concerns through the presentation of their views and opinions and their responses to and deliberations on proposals to the final stage in which the group reached consensus or solved a problem.

Given such understanding, strategies need to be developed in line with the vision, mission, and objective of the organizations, as well as the culturally diverse backgrounds of the members who participate in GVTs. Global leaders of GVTs need to attune their behaviors in order to achieve a cultural fit when confronted with several challenges of culture: national culture, organizational culture, and teamwork culture, because of diversity of the GVT members' characteristics, cultural values, and teamwork dynamics.

Managing Distributed Decision Making in a GVT

The following suggested dos and don'ts offer guidelines for the global leaders of GVTs. They are intended to promote effective decision making when team members are collaborating at a distance. Since culture plays a pivotal role in shaping the way decisions are made within a team, global leaders need to train HC and LC members to work together efficiently and effectively to achieve the best overall performance. Table 16.1 summarizes these guidelines, which are based on a high level of comparison between HC and LC, to illuminate the cultural patterns of decision making within a GVT. The next section explores the dos and don'ts in more detail in terms of four additional cultural dimensions: (1) collectivism versus individualism, (2) neutral versus specific communication styles, (3) time orientation: polychronic versus monochronic, and (4) relationship oriented versus task oriented.

Table 16.1 Comparison of HC and LC Strategies, Approaches, and Mannerisms Employed during Stages of the Decision-Making Process

Cultural Orientation Decision-Making Stage	High Context	Low Context
Problem	• Seldom uses words like *problem* explicitly • Uses a circuitous approach when expressing concerns or issues	• Jumps straight to the point • Clearly states the problem upfront, e.g., "Is there a wireless connection?"
Proposal	• Begins proposals with a formal tone and address, e.g., "Dear all..." • Provides context first using indirect phrases, then expresses views	• Begins proposals with a goal statement and assertion • States points succinctly and clearly
Solution	• Presents decisions in an appreciative and courteous manner	• Informs others of their decisions in a direct and precise manner

The Dos and Don'ts of Cultural Orientation for GVT Leaders

So, what should you do and what should you avoid doing when managing a GVT whose members come from diverse cultural backgrounds? When communicating with GVT members who are culturally disparate, consider the following actions based on four aspects of culture.

1. *Collectivistic versus individualistic*

   High context: HC members are accustomed to a collectivistic society. They incorporate creativity and innovative thinking ("Two minds are better than one") in order to obtain synergies from others. The more ideas that are generated, the more dynamic the deliberation processes, which, in turn, results in higher-quality decisions. Collegiality, dynamism, and cohesiveness are important for collectivistic members so that they feel a strong sense of belonging among the members in GVTs. A GVT leader must be alert and diplomatic when managing discussions so that both types of voices are heard. Once these expectations are clearly established, he or she should strive to develop a personal relationship with each of the members, and he himself or she herself must observe the milestones that are set in order for HC members to follow his or her lead. With both collective and hierarchical relationships established, HC members will feel obligated, as well as motivated, to perform at their best. HC members need guidance to become goal-oriented team players and take responsibility for the tasks that are assigned to them; a good first step is empowering them to make their own decisions. HC members need to avoid staying silent during deliberation because all parties must contribute their individual ingredients. In a GVT work environment, team spirit must be fostered, yet individual empowerment is also necessary. HC members may find it difficult to make decisions without going through their accustomed process of consensus building or referring to the *big boss* for approval. GVT leaders may need to help HC individuals become confident in making decisions and comfortable with being held accountable for the decisions made.

Low context: Team members from an individualistic culture normally ascribe to the concept of a *single-person mind* when coming up with ideas or alternatives, agendas, outcomes, and objectives when pursuing a task. An individualistic team member prefers to stand on his or her own two feet and is perfectly willing to be held accountable for each of the decisions made. GVT leaders must allow this kind of work environment to emerge since, for those from an individualistic culture, the process of decision making takes a straightforward and sequential path. Ideas are generated—as many as possible—and deliberation is carried out as objectively as possible to obtain the best possible outcome. Goal-oriented discussions are much appreciated by such people and are valued more than emotional or relationship-building discussions. The more ideas that spring from individuals on the team, the deeper the discussions become since all decisions can be evaluated in terms of cost–benefit analysis. However, HC cultures need to be educated to be brave in giving their ideas, no matter what, so that each individual is appreciated. LC members, by contrast, need to sustain their individualistic selves so that they can be creative and innovative in their solutions while still striving to be a team player in the GVT context.

2. *Specific versus neutral communication styles*

High context: Since HC team members come from collectivistic cultures, the way they communicate is
largely dependent on the person to whom they are
sending the message. They will communicate differently with those in their in-group (those with whom
they have a strong relationship, close friends, spouse,
and family members) than with those in their out-
group (e.g., strangers or casual acquaintances). HC
individuals also communicate differently based
on the message recipient's level of authority, tend-
ing to be cautious and formal in their speech when
communicating with those above them. For this
reason, GVT leaders will need to employ a context-
dependent manner of communicating. They will
need to take time to discover the implicit and covert
messages hidden in HC team members' statements.
HC individuals tend to employ an indirect style with
people whom they do not know in order to establish a relationship. Their speech takes a formal tone,
more cautious and polite. However, HC individuals
employ a direct communication style when they have
a strong relationship with someone, such as family
members or close friends; they use a less formal tone
and/or terse messages, as they expect the recipient
to understand what they intended to say—to read
their minds—due to their long-standing relationship.
In HC cultures, even simple nonverbal gestures such
as nodding the head can be a clear message to those
whom they are close to.

Low context: LC individuals seldom make a distinction
between the in-group and the out-group. As a result,
their communication style is quite consistent; no one
is treated differently in terms of how they are spoken
to. LC people strive to be exact, clear, and precise

so that messages are delivered efficiently and suc-
cinctly. Messages are articulated in a way that facilitates comprehension of the task to be undertaken;
sometimes, such messages can be perceived by HC
members as brusque, harsh, abrupt, or tactless. GVT
leaders may need to educate HC team members
about the clarity and brevity of messages delivered
by their LC colleagues, explaining that LC people are
clear and brief not out of rudeness or insensitivity but
because they place a higher importance on the message's content than on its context. LC members are
goal oriented since they are individualistic in nature;
their aim is to complete the task that is assigned to
them as efficiently as possible, without regard to any
relationships with other members of the team. GVT
leaders may also need to educate LC team members
on how to express their individualistic ideas in a
more congenial manner, toning down their dominant
voice in order to be perceived properly by their HC
colleagues.

3. *Time orientation: Rigid versus flexible*

   High context: HC individuals have a *polychronic* time
   orientation, meaning that they view time as elas-
   tic and do not perceive urgency unless specifically
   directed so by a superior. At the beginning of a GVT
   project, leaders need to clearly brief HC individuals
   about the rules and procedures so that they understand their roles and tasks. This briefing will give
   HC team members a sense of responsibility and a
   strong motivation to actively support the team-based
   GVT work structure instead of attempting to handle
   their tasks individually. Leaders must also inform HC
   members of punctuality and efficiency expectations
   in terms of adhering to the schedule and milestones,
   including the importance of meeting deadlines. HC

members also need to be educated about concepts of *timeliness* and *time discipline*. Make sure that the time taken to arrive at decisions is well managed and controlled to avoid excessive delays in decision making. Since HC members are used to receiving ideas and instructions in a top–down manner, it is often not easy for them to suggest ideas in the early stages of a project, for the fear that their ideas may be rejected. Openness in attitude and support from the leader and other members will encourage them to participate sooner, and gentle nudges from the leader will help them move forward within the given deadlines.

Given the short time frame of most GVT projects, leaders may need to guide HC members more firmly regarding what needs to be done in the early stages so as to move the project along. Since HC members come from a high power distance culture in which the leader or superior (boss) provides instructions, only then will they feel a sense of urgency to follow through. Leaders will also need to caution their LC members to be patient and to recognize the HC's need for a more bureaucratic process. For decision making in GVTs, it is important to understand the challenges that are presented by different team dynamics when there are members who are relationship oriented rather than task oriented. The relationship-oriented members will tend to have a different view of the task. They believe in ensuring that people can work together cohesively and collegially. Team members must therefore experience a rapport- and trust-building phase in the beginning rather than jumping straight to the work. All of this is time consuming, and, when decisions need to be reached, this happens through a process of idea exchanges and deliberation.

Thus, HC members may not be observant and follow through the timelines set because they need to protect the harmonious work environment among the members.

Low context: LC individuals tend to take a monochronic view of time and employ a sequential way of doing things. Each task has its own process, and the process follows a systematic progression from point A to point B in a timely and efficient manner. For LC individuals, negotiation regarding the timeline is acceptable as long as it is based on clear strategies for how the task will be followed through and completed. For this reason, in certain conditions and under certain circumstances, LC individuals can say "No" to their boss and disagree with his or her decisions, particularly when deadlines are not being met, and they observe deviations from the planned schedule. For LC members, time is money and thus cannot be wasted or neglected. LC team members are sensitive to the need to comply with the conditions, as stipulated in the contract, that clearly establish milestones and outcomes. Timeliness is crucial, and hence any incompatibilities or obstacles need to be avoided or swiftly dealt with at any cost. If a team member encounters problems in the tasks assigned to him or her, LC individuals expect him or her to voice his or her concerns immediately and find solutions to the problem, whether unforeseen or foreseen. Task-oriented team members also tend to start the team process by outlining the procedures and tasks to be accomplished. They will be efficient in providing all the instructions that are needed to get started and normally will not waste any time getting started. In short, GVT leaders need to prepare both HC and LC members to be proactive, as well as reactive, and to align their behaviors with the decisions to be made. If clashes do arise, the deliberation necessary to resolve them may take less time when the members are sensitive to time factors.

4. *Relationship building versus task orientation*

High context: In the early phases of team formation, leaders need to create a warm environment for HC members in order to establish rapport and inculcate trust. HC team members who feel comfortable from the outset will be at ease throughout the rest of the team's work. The glue that bonds a cohesive team is how intensely the members feel for each other and how strong a sense of belonging the members feel, since HC individuals regard relationships as highly important. To create this sense of belonging, GVT leaders can use warm-up sessions or getting-to-know-you sessions during the team's early days. Studies have shown that teams that meet at least once with all members present, whether physically or virtually, perform much better than teams that have no opportunity to meet at all during the span of their project. GVT leaders may want to consider using Skype or other technology so that members have an opportunity to see each other face to face. HC individuals need to feel that their leaders and fellow team members are willing to invest time in getting to know them, so these types of activities are paramount for GVTs since the team may have few chances to meet face to face. Once HC individuals sense interest from their colleagues, they are more willing to move the job along efficiently.

Low context: Although a sense of rapport is important for LC individuals, their priority is more on the task to be accomplished. They emphasize a clear understanding of tasks and outcomes rather than fostering relationships. GVT leaders need to provide LC team members with clear plans, agendas, and milestones so that project goals can be met efficiently and on time. Leaders also need to keep LC members regularly updated on progress. Thus, GVT leaders need to consider both macro and micro levels of planning. LC individuals favor logical thinking and reasoning in their decision making, and task takes priority over relationships, so leaders must foster in their LC members an awareness of the importance of balancing task and relationship building in working with their HC colleagues. LC team members need clear objectives and deadlines, but merely assigning tasks to be carried out without any attention to relationship building will discourage and alienate their HC colleagues.

In a Nutshell

An analysis of the active participants in the WSIS decision-making process clearly showed that HC and LC participants contributed almost equally in all three stages—(1) problem identification, (2) proposal making, and (3) solution. However, when the findings were further explored in terms of *how* the individuals participated in the decision-making process, the two cultural orientations showed differences in strategies, approaches, and mannerisms. At each stage of the decision-making process, the participants exhibited unique behaviors depending on whether they were high or low context. Tables 16.2 and 16.3 summarize the differences in behavior between HC and LC individuals and the related dos-and-don'ts behavior guidelines.

Table 16.2 Distinction of Cultural Values between HC and LC

Cultural Values of High Context	Cultural Values of Low Context
Credibility and trustworthiness. MNCs need to provide all team members with ample background information about each other in order to reduce uncertainties and anxieties about who they will be working with. This information will also help establish a sense of the trustworthiness of the members.	***Reliability and performance.*** Provide clear goals and timelines so that these team members can plan, organize, and coordinate their tasks. Members also need to understand the credibility of their fellow team members, e.g., know something about their past performance, in order to assess their reliability and the quality of their work.
Rapport building. Leaders need to hold a warm-up session—a *getting-to-know-you* session early in the forming of the team, for example, a face-to-face or videoconferencing meeting, to give team members a chance to actually see each other's faces and observe nonverbal cues.	***Task orientation.*** Leaders need to ensure that tasks are clearly identified and delegated to team members. Members need to feel that they have ownership in terms of performing the task assigned to them.
Nonavoidance approach to conflict resolution. Leaders need to intervene when members experience conflicts. Members from an HC culture will use either avoidance or a nonconfrontational strategy once they trust their colleagues.	***Confrontational conflict resolution.*** If conflicts arise, leaders need to think strategically about how to manage them. Oftentimes, the best strategy is to seek a win–win result wherein members deliberate on the best outcome and arrive at a solution that satisfies all parties.

(Continued)

Table 16.2 (Continued)   Distinction of Cultural Values between HC and LC

Cultural Values of High Context	Cultural Values of Low Context
The ability to resolve conflicts in a collegial manner is crucial for maintaining a harmonious relationship. If conflicts arise, members may need an intermediary to arbitrate the issue.	LC culture individuals tend to confront others directly and express their disagreements in an open manner, preferring to deal directly with the affected individual rather than employing a mediator.
Consensus decision making. The decision-making process is based on two key aspects: (1) hierarchical roles and (2) consensus. Thus, HC members generally refer to their leader for a final decision, since they are accustomed to follow bureaucratic procedures or seek the approval of other team members. Members feel more secure receiving instructions on what to do from their leaders, since they will then not be responsible for the success or failure of the outcome.	**Empowerment in decision making.** Since individualistic cultures operate based on self-reliant thinking and autonomous decision making, members of this culture need to feel empowered in decision making. They cannot be told what to do for the sake of following or complying with what others are doing.

Source: Adapted from Mohd Yusof, S.A. & Zakaria, N., *Exploring the State of Discipline on the Formation of Swift Trust within Global Virtual Teams.* Proceedings of the 45th Hawaii International Conference on System Science, Jan. 4–7, Maui, HI, pp. 475–482, 2012.

Table 16.3 High-Level Comparison of Decision-Making Behaviors by Cultural Context

High Context	Low Context
• Begin message using formal salutation or initial greetings • Introduce initial paragraph with compliments, gratitude, and appreciation • Use polite or *padded* words to express feelings or to avoid being frank • Seek approval by asking questions instead of disclosing real intentions or opinions • Write lengthy messages without clear direction or focus (at times)	• Begin message with informal or no salutation • Jump into the subject matter straightaway and express feelings clearly • State opinions first, then soften with polite words (e.g., say thank you but not until late in the message) • Use succinct, brief, assertive, and concise words to make a point • Write lengthy messages with lots of detail when giving instructions or explanations about the assertions made

References

Adler, N.J. 1997. *International Dimensions of Organizational Behavior*, 3rd ed. Cincinnati, OH: South-Western.

Mohd Yusof, S.A. & Zakaria, N. 2012. *Exploring the State of Discipline on the Formation of Swift Trust within Global Virtual Teams*. Proceedings of the 45th Hawaii International Conference on System Science, Jan. 4–7, Maui, HI, pp. 475–482.

Chapter 17

Culture Counts! "It Is Not What You Said, But How You Said It!"

Fatimah was astounded and discouraged when Anthony sent her a message that said, "Your idea is not logical" and then proceeded to suggest another idea—"Option A is a better one!" It was not his rejection of her idea that upset her—after all, in a team, it is totally acceptable for diverse ideas to be brought up—but rather how he said it, snappishly and curtly, with only a few words. "If I were to respond," she thought, "I would say it this way: your idea is good, but there are lots of ways that we can think about the project and its options. We should consider Option A as it has the lesser cost. Perhaps, it would be better if we started by weighing each of the available options to understand the cost and benefit?" Looking back at Anthony's message and the way she herself would have responded, she chuckled. One had an elongated manner with padded words, whereas the other was concise and straight to the point. She began to understand the true influence of culture in a global virtual team (GVT). Even when people were working at a distance, words were an important bridge between team members, but different cultural backgrounds gave them a different sense and aura, altering the working climate. What a shame that she failed to understand the cultural nuances!

Throughout this book, my standpoint, based on my research findings and other related studies, has been clear: *culture does matter.* Culture influences the way that people work, communicate, and collaborate across geographical distances and time. Multinational organizations, especially their GVT leaders, need to pay attention to cultural differences when building a team structure. The readiness of an organization to fully employ the GVT work structure is directly dependent on their ability to develop GVT leaders and teams that are culturally competent. What makes the GVT work structure more challenging is that team members are asked to collaborate with strangers in a virtual space, across geographical boundaries and time zones. Organizations need to nurture leaders who have the right capabilities and competencies to deal with the challenges of working in a virtual collaborative environment. GVT leaders need to develop and hone their skills in all three areas: (1) cognition, (2) emotion, and (3) behaviors—the *CAB* model (refer to Chapter 15 on the intercultural competence model) when they begin to work with and manage teams in the virtual workspace.

Two key questions were asked and answered: (1) how do we develop culturally competent global leaders who are capable of confronting and dealing with multicultural virtual teams? and (2) how do we encourage global leaders to be open to the many idiosyncrasies, the differing emotions, and the unpredictable patterns of thought that may arise from divergent, culturally rooted behaviors? The current challenge for multinational corporations (MNCs) is to build leaders who are wide open in mind, heart, and behavior, as well as competent in their field—they must be willing to embrace all the possibilities inherent in cultural complexity. MNCs must take steps to educate their employees at both the managerial and team-member level, to develop competencies for both leaders and individual contributors in understanding the unique demands and benefits of a team that is composed of people from different cultural backgrounds and working together at a distance. In particular, in order to be successful and effective, GVTs need the guidance of leaders who fully understand the different cultural ways of working in terms of cognition, emotion, and behaviors.

The deeper questions that arise are *why* does culture matter, and *how* does culture matter? Multinational organizations need to address these two fundamental concerns when assigning leaders to high-performing GVTs. Not only team leaders but also team members need to fully develop competencies in all three areas—cognitive, affective, and behavioral (refer to Chapter 15) when they manage team members in the virtual workspace. Cultural values influence all three aspects in various manners due to the GVTs' heterogeneous composition.

For myself, having had the experience of more than 10 years as both a *student-expatriate* in a Western learning context and a *corporate-expatriate* in the Middle Eastern working environment has resulted in such an enduring long-term *life*-learning journey. Hence, cultural competency was built over the years as it grew difficult and challenging—more than I could have ever imagined. When I first arrived in the United States to begin my PhD journey, the exhilaration and the feeling of joy has managed to overcome my fear of living abroad. It was proven that, over the years, my daily face-to-face encounters with cultural diversity have given me golden opportunities to understand why and how people communicate and relate to others. With such deep experiences in the expatriation process, this book offers rich insights into the understanding of how culture impacts online communication.

Despite—or perhaps because of—the astounding advances in computers and communication technologies, people still encounter cultural diversity at a distance. Culture still matters.

In essence, people from different cultural backgrounds use different strategies, approaches, and mannerisms when they communicate. But what is most interesting is that both high- and low-context cultural behaviors showed signs of *switching*—of adaptation or acculturation—in this new GVT environment. Each of the cultural groups seemed to maintain their cultural values and intercultural communication styles, but, at the same time, they also adapted to the cultural values and intercultural communication styles of others. In the cross-cultural and international management literature, many studies have noted that before managers were sent abroad for international assignments, they would be given cross-cultural training to help them better adapt and acculturate to the unfamiliar environment that they would be entering (Zakaria 2000; Adler 1997; Kim 1991; Berry 1990). However, in the case of Civil Society participants, no prior training was given to them because they participated voluntarily. This, and the fact that they came from different parts of the world and belonged to different organizations, made it more challenging to offer any form of cross-cultural training prior to their participation in the WSIS. In this respect, they are *purer* examples of cultural influence on communication because they did not receive any formal cross-cultural training. Yet, over time, they learned to tolerate, be sensitive to, be aware of, and respond accordingly to cultural differences that are encountered during their WSIS participation.

Global leaders need to accustom themselves to the different cultural environments that they encounter and attune their behaviors to take into account the disparate cognitive, affective, and behavioral responses of others. Thus, global leaders managing GVTs need to educate team members to become adaptable in their behavior (flexible and mutable), open their minds (nonjudgmental), and be receptive in their emotions (sympathetic, passionate, and tolerant). In other words, inculcate *switching behaviors* when necessary to reduce culture shock at the individual level and be understood by managers at the organizational level. If full cultural understanding can be achieved, GVT members will celebrate the cultural diversity among them rather than taking it as cultural challenge, thus enhancing rather than impeding their cohesiveness.

In a nutshell, the key purpose of this book was to present a rich description of how different cultural orientations impact communicative and collaborative behaviors, using examples from a study on the WSIS Civil Society decision-making process. By using Hall's high-context versus low-context cultural dimensions, fleshed out with other related cultural dimensions such as individualism–collectivism (Triandis 1988; Hofstede 1980) and task versus relationship oriented (Hall 1976), the preceding chapters, I hope, provide valuable insights and a concrete foundation for the understanding of multidimensional cultural variables as applied in a globally distributed environment.

Misunderstandings stemming from cultural differences will not be alleviated unless and until people learn to be tolerant, appreciative, and aware of and to respond appropriately to such variations. Cairncross (1997) argued strongly that the *death of distance* is the inevitable outcome of computer-mediated communication, whereas Olson and Olson (2000) believe that distance still matters and will continue to pose challenges in a globally distributed collaboration. Barsoux and Schneider (1997) also challenged the myth of the melting pot or global village—i.e., the death of culture. As discussed in this book, there is clear evidence that neither the death of distance nor the death of culture is a reality yet and that differences still exist even in the wired world. What matters, then, is whether these cultural differences will promote or inhibit intelligent, useful, and productive collaboration and communication.

References

Adler, N.J. 1997. *International Dimensions of Organizational Behavior*, 3rd ed. Cincinnati, OH: South-Western.

Barsoux, J.L. & Schneider, S.C. 1997. *Managing Across Cultures*. London: Prentice Hall.

Berry, J.W. 1990. Psychology of acculturation. In J.J. Berman (Ed.), *Nebraska Symposium on Motivation, 1989: Cross-Cultural Perspectives. Current Theory and Research in Motivation*, 37 (pp. 201–234). Lincoln, NE: University of Nebraska Press.

Cairncross, F. 1997. *The Death of Distance: How the Communications Revolution Will Change Our Lives*. Boston: Harvard Business School Press.

Hall, E.T. 1976. *Beyond Culture*. Garden City, NJ: Anchor Books/Doubleday.

Hofstede, G. 1980. *Culture's Consequences: International Differences in Work Related Values*. Beverly Hills, CA: SAGE.

Kim, Y. 1991. Intercultural communication competence. In S. Ting-Toomey & F. Korzenny (Eds.), *Cross-Cultural Interpersonal Communication* (pp. 259–275). Newbury Park, CA: SAGE.

Olson, G.M. & Olson, J.S. 2000. Distance matters. *Human–Computer Interaction*, 15(2 & 3), 139–178.

Triandis, H.C. 1988. Collectivism vs. individualism: A reconceptualization of basic concept in cross-cultural psychology. In G. Verma & C. Bagley (Eds.), *Cross-Cultural Studies of Personality, Attitudes, and Cognition* (pp. 60–95). London: Macmillan.

Zakaria, N. 2000. The effects of cross-cultural training on the acculturation process of the global workforce. *International Journal of Manpower*, 21(6), 492–510.

Index

Printed in the United States
by Baker & Taylor Publisher Services